Metropolitan of Nafpaktos
Hierotheos

The mind
of the Orthodox Church

Translated by
Esther Williams

Birth of the Theotokos Monastery

Original title: Ekklisia & ekklisiastiko fronima
The second edition of the original text has been
used for the translation

Original ©: Metropolitan of Nafpaktos Hierotheos

Translated by Esther Williams, 1998

Cover art: Yannis Yeremtzes

Published by: Birth of the Theotokos Monastery
P.O Box 107, GR-321 00 Levadia-Hellas
tel. & fax: (0268) 31204
e-mail: pelagia@pelagia.org

First edition 1998

ISBN 960-7070-39-9

Contents

5
The mind of the Orthodox Church   119

6
The Catholic way of life   141

Preface to the English edition

The twentieth century, from a Christian point of view, is called the age of Ecclesiology and Eucharistiology because much has been said about what the Church is and what the value of divine Eucharist is. People, disappointed by an individualistic life, seek true social relations which they feel they will find in the Church.

Indeed, man finds true communion with God, men and all creation within the Church and through the Divine Eucharist which is the deepest core of Ecclesiastical life.

At the same time many problems have arisen concerning Church and the ecclesiastical mind-set. Various traditions relating to the Church have created intense speculation.

Many groups of Christians have presented themselves as ecclesiastical ones and many theological opinions have tried to define the true ecclesiastical mind-set. Some Christian groups claim authenticity whereas others mantain that all Christians are branches of a single tree or that Christianity is expressed by and breathes with two lungs. Thus, on the one hand there prevails indiscriminate absolutism and on the other relativity of faith. Indeed this creates a great ecclesiological confusion, a particular ecclesiastical fundamentalism or an ecclesiastical syncretism.

*My visits both to the East and to the West have made
me realise that questions like what the Church is which
Church expresses authenticity, what exactly constitutes
the ecclesiastical mind-set are really very interesting and
modern. Many people, disappointed by various Christian
denominations, are seeking out the Orthodox Church of
Revelation, of the Fathers, of the Ecumenical Councils,
of the martyrs and of the saints.*

*However, due to the ecclesiological confusion which
exists even within the local Orthodox ecclesiastical communities they do not find what they are looking for.*

*And this arises because secularization also troubles
many Orthodox communities, because either a dogmatic
minimalism or a dogmatic maximalism prevails, or even
more so an ecclesiological Monophycitism or an ecclesiological Nestorianism prevails.*

*This present book which is now published in English
consists of nine talks addressed to the Catechists (both
clergy and laity) of the Holy Archdiocese of Athens, Greece
and aimed at locating various ecclesiological problems,
without, of course, exhausting the subject. Nevertheless
they set out the foundation of Ecclesiology according to
the Fathers and they try to help us avoid the temptations
of so called "Baptismal theology" and of "dogmatic syncretism" as well as avoid the dangers of legalism and
secularization.*

*I feel it is my duty to thank Mrs Esther Williams who
has translated the book, both motivated by her thirst for
true Orthodox life, which she found many years ago, when
she entered the Orthodox Church living within it in simplicity, humility and deep faith and also has the selfless
and indispensable support of Ms Rosslyn Nicholas. I also
thank Ms Effie Mavromichali who has compared and*

checked the English translation with the greek text with enthousiasm and knowledge and has made some accurate observations.

Thanks are due to the Holy Monastery of the Birth of Theotokos which has the zeal and love for publishing and distributing this kind of books.

My thanks are also addressed to all English-speaking Orthodox Christians who encourage the translation of such texts and contribute to their circulation out of their love for Orthodoxy. Fr. Nicholas Palis, priest of the Church of the Dormition of the Virgin, Aliquippa Pensylvania, occupies a significant place among them.

I glorify God in Trinity for this new translation, I express my gratitude to the Holy, God-seeing Fathers who handed to us the Truth of Revelation through their struggles and martyrdoms.

I praise all those who contribute to the strengthening of Orthodox life and teaching.

I also pray that all of us be worthy of becoming disciples of the Holy Apostles and Fathers as well as confessors of authentic Orthodox faith and life.

Written in Nafpaktos on June 29, 1998, feast of St. Peter and Paul chief among the Apostles

Introduction

All the Christians, Clerical and lay, have often become aware that if there is a burning topic and a great contemporary need, it is the need to acquire the mind* of the Church. Our mind should be permeated by the mind of the Church. Our thought, life, mode of living, our desire, our will should be altered by the good alteration effected by the life of the Church.

The Apostle Paul urges: "Let this mind be in you which was also in Christ Jesus" (Phil. 2. 5). But since the Church is not a human organisation, but the holy and blessed Body of Christ, therefore we too are commanded to think with the catholic mind of the Church and be animated by the life of the Church, not to do anything apart from its life and teaching.

This is connected with two facts. One, that there are many Christians today who do not have the mind of the Church, that is to say, their mind is on "earthly things" (Phil. 3,19). Their mind is estranged from the mind of the Church, it is simply worldly. Their life is not in tune with the mind of the Church. The other fact is that acquiring the mind of the Church is related to the "making" of a man, which is con-

---

* The word mind denotes the way of thinking and consequently the way of acting as a member of the Orthodox Church *nected with his deification. In so far as the man has an unclean and darkened nous, he is an infant and a baby. To the extent that he grows in illumination of his nous, he also is made a man, which means that he is "Christified" and "made Church".*

In this perspective we can look at the Apostle Paul's words: "When I was a child, I spoke as a child, I understood as a child, I thought as a child; but when I became a man, I put away childish things" (1 Cor. 13, 11). If this passage is associated with what the Apostle said before and after it – where he was speaking of the "perfect" in relation to what is "in part" and about seeing God "face to face" in relation to "seeing in a mirror dimly" – then we can understand that the mind of the Church is connected with man's spiritual fulfilment, which consists in partaking of the purifying, illuminating and deifying energy of God.

A great deal is being said today about acquiring the mind of the Church. Sometimes, however, we do not know just what the mind of the Church is. We identify it with a blind obedience to some general laws or else we connect it with outward things. We usually think that it is the mind of the Church when the others accept us. But if they dare to cast doubt on our actions, we consider that they lack the mind of the Church. Thus we divide people as being of the Church or not, by external things and by characteristics which we construct according to our passions.

I shall try to study this topic within the Tradition of the Church. The chapters which follow and which are homilies that I gave to the Catechists of the Holy Archbishopric of Athens in the "Seminar" for further training of catechists in 1989-1990, as Director of Youth of the Archbishopric of Athens, with the blessing of his grace the Ever memorable Seraphim, Lord Archbishop of Athens and All Greece. I do not the diagnosis of the mind of the Church, and they raise questions. An analysis had to be made as to what the Church is, in order for us to see the real dimensions of the mind of the Church. Some repetitions were necessary, because the mystery of the Church is single and cannot be split into absolutely water-tight compartments.

May the circulation of this new book stimulate us to experience the mind of the Church. It is the greatest pastoral necessity today. However, it will not be the result of a mental exercise, but a fruit of our spiritual rebirth from a deified spiritual father, since the Church is not an object of study, but a reality which we live, our mother which nourishes us and fills us with life.

Written on the Friday of the
Akathist hymn 30 March, 1990,
the day of remembrance of our
holy Father John of Sinai.

Archimandrite Hierotheos S. Vlachos

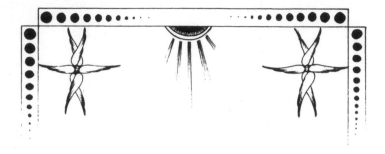

1

Origin and revelation
of the Church

Origin and revelation
of the Church

Through the centuries there have appeared many heretical teachings which distorted the revealed truth, and which the holy Fathers confronted "with the slingstone of the Spirit", that is to say, by the power of the Holy Spirit. And this is so because the holy Fathers were the bearers of the pure Tradition of the Church.

Among these heresies are those of Arianism, the pneumatomachs who fought against the spirit, the Nestorians, the monophysites, the monothelites, the iconoclasts, etc. All these heresies refer chiefly to the Person of Christ, but also to that of the Holy Spirit, and of course they disturb the foundations of man's salvation. For if Christ is not consubstantial with the Father, but is God's first creature, and if the Holy Spirit is not true God, man's salvation is put in doubt, the possibility of deification is cut off.

Later, during the fourteenth century yet another heresy appeared, which was expressed by Barlaam and based on rationalism. If Barlaam's heretical teaching had prevailed, the method of the Orthodox way towards deification, which is hesychasm*, would in fact have ended in agnosticism.

---

* Certain key words of Orthodox spirituality are listed in a glossary and are indicated with an asterisk where they first occur in the translation.

The question being asked is whether there are heresies today as well. The answer is not hard to find, because all of us are being made witnesses of the fact that there are indeed heretics now, descendants of the great heretics, and there are heretical teachings being expressed, perhaps not deliberately, by some who believe, among other things, that they are really members of the Church of Christ. And indeed all of us in our ignorance and lack of learning, may have some erroneous views about God and the way of salvation, but we must struggle never to become heresiarchs or descendants of the great heretics who have appeared in the history of the Church.

Besides, all the heretics were members of the Church for a time, even Clergy, and were active in it. The Apostle Paul's prophecy applies here: "Also from among yourselves men will rise up, speaking perverse things, to draw away the disciples after themselves" (Acts 20,30).

All the heresies distort the ecclesiology as well. Since the Church is the Body of Christ, every alteration in the teaching about Christ, about the Holy Spirit, about the way to man's salvation also has ecclesiological consequences.

It can be said that if there is a great heresy today, it is the so-called ecclesiological heresy. And this should be confronted by the Pastors of the Church. There is great confusion today about what the Church is and who are its true members. We confuse or identify the Church with other human Traditions, we think that the Church is fragmented and split up, and furthermore, we are ignorant of the Church's way of salvation. Thus it is in confusion about this great theme.

In the chapters to follow we shall attempt to examine the subject of the Church from different angles, and we shall try to see what the holy Fathers say about the Church.

I think that this will help us to acquire the genuine mind of the Orthodox Church, which is essential for our salvation.

1. Etymology of the word 'Ekklesia' (Church)

But before I proceed to elaborate the subject of the "origin and revelation of the Church", I would like us to take a look at the etymology of the word "Ekklesia", because it will help us to understand better what is going to be said further on.

The word 'Ekklesia' derives from the verb meaning 'to call out' 'call', 'call together', 'gather together'. Thus 'Church' means a gathering of people, a congregation.

We can also find the word in this meaning in ancient Greece with reference, for example, to the 'ekklesia' of a municipality, a gathering of the citizens to discuss various concerns which they had.

Also in holy Scripture, in both the Old and New Testaments, there is repeated reference to the 'Ekklesia' as an assembly. The phrases 'ekklesia of saints', 'ekklesia of laity' etc., are often used in the Old Testament. But in the New Testament we also have abundant use of the word with a deeper content, since through the incarnation of Christ the Church is not a gathering of people, but the Body of Christ. Thus it acquires a deeper meaning. I would like to cite a few examples.

Christ said to the Apostle Peter, who confessed His divinity: "You are Peter, and on this rock I will build My Church, and the gates of Hades shall not prevail against it" (Matt. 16,18). The rock ('petra') on which the Church is supported is the confession that Christ is the Son of God. The Apostle Paul repeatedly speaks of the Church as the Body of Christ. This passage from the letter to the Ephesians is characteristic: "And He put all things under His feet, and gave Him to be head over all things to the Church, which is His Body, the fullness of Him Who fills all in all" (Eph. 1, 22-23). The members, the Christians who make up the membership of a concrete eucharistic community, are also characterised as the Church. The Church possesses the whole truth, because the whole revelation of God has been given to it. The Apostle Paul says: "Church of the living God, the pillar and ground of the truth" (1 Tim. 3, 15).

The word 'Church' is also used in these meanings in the teaching of the holy Fathers and in the Worship. According to St. Kyril of Jerusalem, it is called the Church "because it calls forth and assembles together all men". And St. John Chrysostom says characteristically "in the multitude of the faithful, the Church". On another subject I shall be developing further what the multitude of the faithful means. In any case I must call to mind here the teaching of St. John Chrysostom that the Church is not a wall and a roof, but living and life.

The Church is presented in many liturgical texts as a gathering, and especially as a eucharistic place, because the Eucharist is the deepest expression of the Church. I would like us to look at a characteristic passage from the Liturgy of the apostolic era as it has been preserved in the Teaching of the Twelve Apostles. At the end of the Eucharist when the Celebrant of the eucharistic gathering took the bread into his hands, he prayed: "We thank Thee, our Father, for the life and knowledge which Thou gavest us through Thy Son Jesus". And then he spoke an amazing prayer "Just as this fraction was scattered over the granaries and, gathered together, became one, so may Thy Church be gathered from the ends of the earth into thy kingdom". The bringing together of many grains of wheat and the preparation of the bread is an image pointing to the gathering of all the faithful into the Kingdom of God.

Among the expressions which are to be found in the liturgical texts and show exactly what the Church is, there is also the expression that the Church is "a holy people" or "communion of saints". The people of God is not only the Clergy or only the laity, but the unity of Clergy, monks and laity, and this unity is in Christ. 'In Christ' means that members of the Church are all those who are united with Christ, all who are actually members of the Body of Christ through the sacramental and ascetic life, all who are baptised and confirmed in the faith, according to the teaching of St. Symeon the New Theologian.

This unity is shown clearly on the holy paten. In the middle there is the lamb of God, Christ Himself, on His right the portion of the Theotokos* and on his left the portions of the saints, and in front the Bishop of the local Church with the living and those who lie asleep whom the priest mentions during the proskomidi. St. Symeon of Thessaloniki, speaking of the holy paten, says: "God among gods who are deified by Him Who is God by nature". Christ is God by nature and the saints are deified by grace through Him Who is God by nature. The assembly of the faithful is expressed once more during the Sacrament of the divine Eucharist.

I shall not concern myself further with this point here, because the subject of who are the true members of the Church will concern us in other sections and other chapters.

2. Origin and revelation of the Church

Many of us have the notion that the Church was created on the day of Pentecost, that is to say, when the Holy Spirit descended into the hearts of the Apostles. And of course we could say that Pentecost is the birthday of the Church from the point of view that it was then that the Church became the Body of Christ. It acquired substance. However, the beginning and existence of the Church is to be found in the time before Pentecost.

Professor John Karmiris states that there are three phases in the emergence of the Church. The first is the creation of the angels and men, the second is the life of Adam in Paradise, but also the period of the Old Testament, and the third phase of the Church is the incarnation of Christ. Indeed the full revelation of the Church will take place at the Second Coming of Christ[1].

Let us look more analytically at these periods of the Church, for then in some way we can grasp the mystery of the Church and gain a deeper awareness of our being and scope.

---

1. – John Karmiris: Orthodox Ecclesiology, Athens 1973.
   – Ibid.: Religious and Ethical Encyclopedia, pub. Martinos, vol.5, p. 465f
   – Gregory Larentzakis: "Views about the pre-existence of the Church in Orthodox and Roman Catholic theology", in the periodical 'Gregory Palamas', no.623, p.240-255 and no.624, p. 295-312, 1971
   – Protopriest Gregory Metallinos: "The Church", ed. Orthodoxos Typos, Athens 1980

a) The beginning of the Church

It is a teaching of the holy Fathers that with the creation of the angels we have the emergence of the first Church. And it can be seen in the writings of the Fathers of the Church that the angels too are members of the Church. Moreover, God the Father is the creator of "all things visible and invisible". Among the invisible are listed the angels, who sing in praise of God. In the book of Job this witness is preserved: "when the stars were born all the angels in a loud voice sang in praise of me" (Job 38,7). Thus, before the creation of the sensible world there were angels, who sang in praise of God for the creation. And, to be sure, this means that the angels were the first to be created by God.

The fact that the angels are members of the Church, since they sing in praise of God, appears in many troparia. I would like to mention one of these: "By Thy Cross, O Christ, one flock came into being, of angels and men, and one Church: heaven and earth rejoice; O Lord, glory to Thee". Angels and men belong to the same Flock, to the same Church after the incarnation of Christ. But this means that this unity also existed in the life before the fall. In the teaching of the holy Fathers it is clear that the 'last things' are like the first and like those in between, because we cannot speak of eschatology apart from the life of man before the fall and apart from the deification of the saints already even before the Second Coming of Christ. Besides, according to the teaching of St. Gregory Palamas and other saints, the vision of the uncreated Light is the substance of the good things to come, this very Kingdom of God.

In Holy Scripture it is taught repeatedly that the angels constitute the first church. The Apostle Paul writing to the

Hebrews says: "You have come to Mount Zion to the heavenly Jerusalem, the city of the living God. You have come
to thousands upon thousands of angels in joyful assembly" (Heb. 12, 22-23).

Thus the first Church, of which the angels were members, was spiritual. Clement of Rome says that the Church
"from above, first, created spiritual before the sun and
moon, and being spiritual, it was made manifest in the flesh
of Christ". And St. John Chrysostom, urging silence during the services in the Temple, said with his characteristic
expressiveness: "For the Church is not a barber's shop nor
a perfume shop nor any other workshop in the markets,
but a place of angels, a place of archangels, Kingdom of
God, heaven itself". Chrysostom says further that the Christian should have in mind that in the Church, especially
during divine Worship, there is a "choir of angels".

The angels are members of the Church because they
too are created by God. Everything created is a creature,
since it has a beginning. The angels not only were created
by God, but they have also been perfected by the power
and energy of the Holy Spirit. Therefore St. John of Damaskos writes: "All the angels were created by the Word
and were perfected by the sanctification of the Holy Spirit, taking part according to the standing and rank of their
illumination and grace".

This view that the angels are members of the Church is
very moving. It is a witness of the saints, because many of
them, like St. Spiridon, saw angels worshipping with them
during the Divine Liturgy. And this offers another dimension to the spiritual life.

The first Church was completed with the creation of man,
Adam and Eve, and their being placed in Paradise. So it is
that men sang praises to the glory of God with the angels.

b) The Church in the Old Testament

Adam and Eve lived an angelic life in Paradise. They were in the state of illumination of the nous, which is the first degree of the vision of God. They had communion with God.

According to the teaching of the holy Fathers, Paradise was tangible and intelligible. This is said by St. Gregory the Theologian and is repeated by St. John of Damaskos. The tangible Paradise was a particular place, and the intelligible Paradise was the communion and union of man with God. And of course the two Paradises interpenetrated, in the sense that the Paradise of Eden was receiving God's uncreated energy.

St. Gregory of Sinai gives us an interpretation of Paradise, which was the second period of the Church. He writes that Paradise was twofold, "tangible and intelligible, namely that in Eden and that of grace". About the Paradise of Eden he says that it was not completely incorruptible nor completely corruptible, but it had been created "between corruption and incorruption". The trees that were in Paradise had their natural cycle of flower-bearing, fruit-bearing and the falling of the fruits. When the ripe fruits fell to the ground, and when the trees decayed "they became fragrant dust and did not have a stench like the plants of the world". There was the natural recycling in the trees and plants, but since Adam had not yet lost the grace of God and therefore the deep darkness had not fallen on the whole creation, there was no decay, a stench did not prevail. There was the whole cycle, but not also decay and stench. And this was so, as St. Gregory of Sinai says, "because of the great wealth and holiness of the ever-abounding grace there".

Through Adam's fall, man's communion with God, with himself, and with the whole creation was broken. Thus man was wearing the garments of the skin of decay and mortality, and of course the whole creation fell into darkness, and "has been groaning as in the pains of childbirth right up to the present time" (Rom. 8,22).

However, in spite of Adam's fall, the Church does not disappear completely. Man struggles to restore his communion with God and attempts it through various forms of religion, because he has lost the true mindfulness and real knowledge of God.

In the Old Testament there were righteous men, like the Judges, Prophets and saints, who were blessed with divine revelation and vision. They saw God. And since the vision of God in the teaching of the Fathers of the Church is identified with deification and man's communion with God, we say that in the Old Testament the small remnant is preserved, the Church exists.

In what follows I would like to cite some patristic passages which clarify this truth.

We know from the teaching of the saints that all the manifestations of God in the Old Testament are manifestations of the Word, the Second Person of the Holy Trinity. The difference between the manifestations in the Old and New Testaments is that in the former we have manifestations of the unincarnate Word, while in the New Testament we have manifestations of the incarnate Word.

Speaking on this theme, St. Gregory the Theologian, in his homily on the Maccabees, says that the saints in the Old Testament knew Christ, and calls this saying mysterious and ineffable. He says that before the incarnation of Christ no one was perfected without faith in Christ. "For the Word spoke boldly later in His own times, but He was also known before to the pure in mind, as is clear from many held in honour before that". And indeed he says of the Maccabees that we should not scorn them with the justification that they lived and acted before the cross, "but that they should be praised in accordance with the cross and are worthy of honour by their words". The righteous men in the Old Testament acted according to the teaching of the cross and, essentially, they experienced the mystery of the Cross.

St. John Chrysostom, referring to the righteous men of the Old Testament, says that they too belong to the Body of Christ, because "they too knew Christ". Besides, by His incarnation Christ, as Chrysostom says again, "assumed flesh of the Church". The Body of Christ is one and the Church is one. Chrysostom asks: "What is one body?" And he himself answers characteristically: "The faithful of the world everywhere, those who are, those who have been and those who will be. And again, those who were well pleasing to God before Christ's appearance are one body". Moreover, both the Old and New Testaments are inspired by the same Spirit. Therefore the holy Father says again: "The Old and New Testaments are of the same spirit, and the same Spirit that uttered the voice then has spoken here". And this is seen from the fact that the holy Fathers interpreted the Old Testament, just as they also interpreted the New Testament, they spoke about dogmatic topics with arguments from the Old Testament as well as Old Testament persons whom they presented as examples of perfection. A characteristic example is St. Gregory of Nyssa, who, in order to present an example of a perfect spiritual man, analysed the person and work of Moses. The life of Moses is a model of the spiritual life for every Christian.

But also the champion of Orthodoxy, Athanasios the

Great, presents a teaching of the same kind. He writes that the Holy Spirit is one Who, both then, that is, in the Old Testament, and now, sanctifies and comforts those receptive to being comforted. "As one and the very Logos Son Himself leading the worthy ones into adoption even then. For they were sons also in the Old Testament, but if adopted by the Son, not by another".

Thus there was a Church in the Old Testament as well, in spite of the fall of man. Members of this Church were the righteous and the Prophets, who had the grace of God. This is confirmed by the sacramental practice of the Church. All the sacraments which we perform in the Christian Church have reference to the Sacraments and rites of the Old Testament. We can take the Sacrament of marriage as an example. During the this ceremony, in the prayers which we address to God, we ask Him to bless the couple, as He blessed Abraham and Sarah, Jakob and Rebecca, etc. Then the words "bless them, our Lord God as Thou didst bless Abraham and Sarah" show that the blessing is the same. We observe this in all the sacraments. Actually there is one difference which we shall see in the next section, about the third period of the Church, that of the incarnation of Christ. In any case, here it is to be noted that the Church exists also in the Old Testament.

c) The Church in the New Testament

With the incarnation of Christ we have the manifestation of the Church. The Church becomes the Body of Christ and acquires its Head, Who is Christ. Let us recall the passage in Clement of Rome which we mentioned before, according to which the Church was "first created spiritual from above, before the sun and moon, and being spiritual, was manifested in the flesh of Christ". And St. Maximos the Confessor says characteristically: "the mystery hidden from the ages and from the generations, was now made manifest by the true and perfect incarnation of the son of God, who united our nature to Himself inseparably and unconfusedly".

By the incarnation of Christ the human nature which Christ assumed was made divine, and through this the Christians, the members of the Church, are full members of the Body of Christ.

Here too we find the difference between the New and Old Testaments. At this point there needs to be an explanation, so that we can place things in their true dimensions.

We said before that in the Old Testament the holy Prophets attained deification. For according to the teaching of the holy Fathers, and of St. Gregory Palamas as well, the vision of God, which is the vision of the uncreated Light, comes through man's deification. The man is deified and thus made worthy of seeing the uncreated glory of God. Man cannot see God by his own powers. In the Church we sing: "in Thy light shall we see light". Thus the vision of God comes from within, not from outside, that is to say it takes place through man's deification. It is not a matter of seeing external things and signs. This is a crucial point in patristic theology. In this sense the holy Fathers speak of the friends of the Cross who existed in the Old Testament, and say that the righteous ones of the Old Testament, such as Abraham, Moses, etc., experienced the mystery of the Cross.

However, this deification of the Prophets was temporary, because death had not yet been abolished, and that is why they were brought to Hades and the vision was outside the Body of the divine human Christ. This is seen in the difference between the experience of the Apostles at the Transfiguration of Christ and the experience which they themselves had on the day of Pentecost.

At the Transfiguration the Disciples saw the uncreated glory of the Holy Trinity in the human nature of the Logos. In order for them to attain this great experience, they had to have been transfigured beforehand: "they were changed in turn, and they saw the change". This change of the Disciples is identical with deification. Through deification they attained the vision of God, and therefore in the patristic teaching the vision of God is connected with men's deification. However, although the vision of the uncreated glory of God came from within, that is to say, through deification, nevertheless the Light which poured forth from the Divine human Body of Christ was external to the holy Apostles, since they had not yet become members of the Body of Christ.

At Pentecost we have this great gift. The Disciples saw the glory of God inwardly, that is to say through deification, but also from within the Divine-human Body of Christ, since with the coming of the Holy Spirit they had become members of the Body of Christ. At Pentecost the Body of Christ was not external to the Apostles, as it was at the Transfiguration, but internal, in the sense that the Disciples had become members of the Body of Christ and as members of the Body of Christ they were worthy of this experience[2].

With the incarnation of Christ the Church became a Body. The Sacraments of the New Testament are different

---

2. For further analysis see in Archimandrite Hierotheos Vlachos: Anatolika, vol.1, p.398 f.

in this way from the Sacraments of the Old Testament. They are performed within the Church, which is the Body of Christ, and they have reference to and conclude in the Sacrament of the divine Eucharist, in which we eat and drink the Body and Blood of Christ. Through the Sacrament of marriage God's blessing is offered, as in the Old Testament, but at the same time it is linked with the Sacrament of the Divine Eucharist as well, and thus the relationship of the couple is not only a biological unity, but also an ecclesiastical, eucharistic unity. This has great significance and gives a different perspective and a different authentication to the Sacraments.

d) The perpetuity of the Church

By his incarnation Christ assumed human nature, and indeed human nature was united with the divine nature immutably, without confusion, inseparably, unchangeably and indivisibly. They are never separated. They remain united forever.

Thus the Church will exist also after the Second Coming of Christ and we shall be able to speak of the perfect manifestation of the Church. This is said from the point of view that the saints are already tasting the last things, because, as we said in the beginning, the last things in the Church are not isolated from the first and intermediate things. Living in the Church, we reach the state of Adam in Paradise before the fall, and we ascend still higher, because we attain communion and unity with Christ, united in His Divine-human Body, having become members of His Body.

The saints from now on are enjoying the glory of God, and therefore St. Symeon the New Theologian says that those who have been granted the vision of the uncreated Light are not waiting for the Second Coming, because they are already experiencing the Kingdom of God.

Besides, the Kingdom of God is not something created, nor is it an earthly reality, but, as St. Gregory Palamas teaches, participation in the Kingdom of God is identified and linked with the vision of the uncreated Light.

However, there will be a continuous perfecting of this participation in the glory of God. This is important, because if the future life is a stationary condition, then it will not have fullness. St. Gregory of Sinai says characteristically: "It is said that in the age to come, the Angels and saints ever increase in gifts of grace and never abate their longing for further blessings. No lapse or veering from virtue to vice takes place in that life".

And St. Gregory Palamas, referring to this point, speaks of the continual development in deification, in man's continual perfecting. Asking: "Do not the saints progress infinitely in the vision of God in the age to come?" He gives the answer himself: "In everything it is clearly to infinity". Indeed he makes use of the case of the Angels who, according to the teaching of St. Dionysios the Areopagite, become increasingly receptive "to the clearest illumination". God is infinite and therefore grants His grace abundantly and plentifully. St. Gregory Palamas asks: "What way is left but for the sons of the age to come, to advance in this to infinity, admitted from grace to grace and patiently making the tireless ascent?" This will be because, according to the same saint, "the previous grace empowers them to partake of greater things".

Of course, in saying these things, we must emphasise that it is not a matter of the restoration of all things, a teaching which was not adopted by the Church, but of the development and perfection of the saints, those who during their lives partook of the purifying, illuminating and deifying energy of God. For those men who did not participate even in the purifying grace of God, that is to say, did not enter the stage of repentance, this good development will not take effect. Furthermore, the passages which we mentioned speak of the saints who acquired the grace of God, and therefore in them the previous grace is empowering towards participation in greater things. Therefore the memorial services which the Church performs for those who have died also have this aim. They help the person in his perfecting, because, according to the teaching of the saints, "this is the perfect unending perfection of the perfect ones".

In this sense we can say that after the Second Coming of Christ we shall have a more complete manifestation of the glory of God. And it is in this perspective that we should interpret the teaching of the saints that now we have as a pledge a taste of the good things of the Kingdom of God.

3. Conclusion

After all that has been reported we must end with a few conclusions, without, of course, having exhausted this great theme.

a) Only in Christ is there salvation. Since the saints of the Old Testament saw the unincarnate Word and the saints of the New Testament saw and see the incarnate Word and have close communion with Him, this means that man's salvation takes place only through Christ. And of course since Christ is the Second Person of the Holy Trinity and salvation is a common action of the Trinitarian God, it means that we are saved when we have communion with the Holy Trinity, when the grace of the Trinitarian God enters our being, when "the grace of our Lord Jesus Christ and the love of God the Father and the communion of the Holy Spirit" are with us.

b) The Church is not a human organisation, but a Divine-Human Organism. It is not a human corporation, but the Divine-human Body of Christ. The source of the Church is this God Himself. It is not men's invention, it is not a fruit and result of men's social need, but it is the sole place of man's salvation. That is to say, the impression is created that men made the Church in order to be able to survive in such difficult and tragic social conditions of life. But, as we explained before, the source of the Church is God Himself, and man's salvation takes place within it. Clement of Alexandria observes: "for just as it is a work of his will and is called the world, so also the salvation of men is his will and this is called the church". And this means that the Church will never cease to exist, in spite of such difficult and unfavourable circumstances.

c) In the Church all the problems are solved. We are not speaking of an abstract Christianity which we link with an ideology, but of a Church which is a communion of God and man, of angels and men, of earthly and heavenly, of man and world. The Church is "a meeting of heaven and earth". Peace, justice, etc., are not simply some social conventions, but gifts which are given in the Church. Peace as well as justice and all the other virtues, such as love etc. are experiences of the Church. In the Church we experience the real peace, justice and love, which are essential energies of God.

d) The Church is the Body of Christ, which has Christ as its head, and the members of the Church are members of the Body of Christ. Members of the Church exist in all the ages and will exist until the end of all time. And when members of the Church cease to exist, the end of the world will come. Thus we are living with many people. The people of God manifest the true communion. As we said at the beginning, on the paten during the Liturgy there are many people. They are the Panagia*, the Angels, the Prophets, the holy Fathers, the great martyrs, and, in general, the witnesses of the faith, the saints and ascetics, the living and the dead who have a share in the purifying, illuminating and deifying uncreated energy of God. We are not alone. We are not "foreigners and aliens, but fellow citizens with the saints and members of God's household" (Eph. 2,19).

The greatest gift of grace which we have is that we belong to the Church. The greatest gift is that we are in this great Family. We should value this gift, we should feel very deeply moved and struggle to remain in the Church, experiencing its sanctifying grace and showing by our lives that we are in its place of redemption and sanctification. Thus we shall also have the great gift of the "blessed ending", when we are granted to lie asleep "in the midst of the Church".

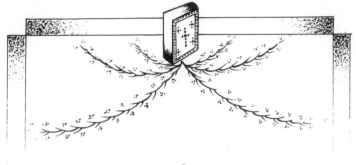

2

"Definition" and characteristics
of the Church

"Definition" and characteristics
of the Church

In the preceding chapter, entitled "Origin and revelation of the Church", we saw that the beginning of the Church is God Himself, that the Church begins with the creation of the angels and man, continuing in the Old Testament, and that through the incarnation of the Word of God the Church becomes the Body of Christ. We can speak of the Church in this sense.

In the present chapter we shall look at the Church in the perspective of the incarnation of the Word of God, that is to say, we shall say more about the Church as the Body of Christ.

1. The Church as a mystery

First it should be underlined that the Church is a mystery. Linked with Christ and being His Body, it is not a human organisation, but a Divine-human Organism. At the same time the Church is not, as is usually said, the mystical Body of Christ, because the Christians, who are the members of the Church, are the real members of the Body of Christ. So we cannot speak of a mystical body, which is abstract and apprehended spiritually, but of the real Body of Christ.

The fact that the Church is the Body of Christ does not mean that it is ontologically identified with Christ, the Second Person of the Holy Trinity. Nor is the divine nature in Christ to be identified with the human nature, because each nature retains its properties. Thus also the Church is not identified ontologically with its Head, but it is closely linked with Christ.

In any case, even if the Church is not the mystical, but the real Body of Christ, it is still a mystery and what takes place in the Church is a mystery. This means that we cannot investigate and concern ourselves with the Church through reasoning and the senses, nor can we interpret it by some outward characteristics.

It is usually said that the Church has seven Sacraments. Without denying this fact, I would like to emphasise that this is a later statement and that in any case there is variation in the history of the number of Sacraments. The holy Fathers think chiefly of three Sacraments, those of Baptism, Chrismation and the divine Eucharist. The Sacrament of Baptism is called an introductory Sacrament, because it introduces us into the new life, into the Body of Christ. Holy Chrismation is the so-called Baptism of the Spirit, giving us the possibility for the grace of Baptism to work within us. And the Sacrament of the divine Eucharist deifies a person through his reception of the Body and Blood of Christ. All the other Sacraments (priesthood, marriage, unction, confession) are closely connected with these three, presupposing the Sacraments of Baptism and Chrismation and being completed in the Sacrament of the divine Eucharist.

But if we give careful attention, we will discover that

all the Sacraments are closely connected with the stages of the spiritual life, namely purification of the heart, illumination of the nous and deification. Of course when we speak of stages, we should not think from a human perspective, but in relation to partaking of the uncreated grace of God. And the holy Fathers are clear when they speak of categories of people who partake of the purifying, illuminating and deifying energy of God. One can state that a sacrament is participation in the uncreated grace of God. And since participation in the uncreated grace takes place according to the person's spiritual condition, we say that there are three sacraments in the Church: purification, illumination and deification. We call God's uncreated energy purifying, illuminating and deifying in accordance with the effects, the results, for according to St. John of Damaskos "energy, active, action and acting are all different things". Thus the Sacraments which we have in the Church (Baptism, Chrismation, divine Eucharist, priesthood, marriage, confession, unction) are manifestations of the purifying, illuminating and deifying energy of God. And of course they are closely connected with these energies. When they are separated they lose their real value.

In any case, what happens in the Church is a mystery. And this is because the Church is not a human organisation, nor is it, I could say, a religious organisation which satisfies some religious needs, but it is the real Body of Christ, the Head of which is Christ.

2. "Definition" of the Church

What has been said by way of introduction shows that there are some problems about the definition of the Church. Therefore of course I would like to emphasise that it is on sufferance that we called this chapter "Definition" of the Church. I think that with what follows this will become more clear[1].

In earlier times various definitions of what the Church is had been formulated by some theologians. The definitions themselves move in approximately the following framework. The Church is all of the people who believe in Christ, who confess that Jesus Christ is the Head, He is their God and Lord, who have the same faith and confession, who are sanctified through the holy Sacraments, who are directed towards salvation by the Pastors who have unbroken apostolic succession etc.

Such definitions have been influenced by Western handbooks about the Church, because later it was discovered that we cannot give a definition of the Church, since not even the holy Fathers do it. Therefore we observe that in the patristic teaching there are no definitions of the Church. I repeat once again that more recent theologians have made clear that the definitions of the Church are derived from the scholastic theology of the West.

In holy Scripture and in the patristic writings what is said mostly is that the Church is the Body of Christ and a communion of deification. That the Church is the Body of Christ is seen in Holy Scripture, especially in the Epistles of the Apostle Paul. In the teaching of St. Gregory Pala-

---

1. John Karmiris: Orthodox Ecclesiology, Athens 1973.
   - Ibid.: Encyclopedia of Religion and Ethics, vol.5, p.474f
   - George Florovsky: Bible, Church, Tradition, USA 1972.
   - Archim. Justin Popovich: Orthodox Church and Ecumenism
   - Prot. George Metallinos: The Church. Athens 1980
   - Hieromonk Artemios Rantosavlievich: The mystery of salvation according to St. Maximos the Confessor

mas the phrase "communion of deification" is also added, because it shows what is the purpose of the Church. The Church's purpose is to lead man to deification. When we release the Church from this purpose, we will make it more an ideology, a religious and human organisation. And we know very well that there is a great difference, I would say a chaotic one, between ideology and Church. The former has ideas, while the Church has life, a life which is an overcoming of death.

The Church, then, is the Body of Christ and a communion of deification. Christ is the Head of the Church and the Church is His glorious Body. And just as we cannot give a definition of Christ, who is its Head, except to say that He is the Divine-Human Christ, so also we cannot give an adequate definition of the Church, except that it is the Body of the Divine-human Christ. Furthermore, as the Greek word indicates, a definition is a limitation. We cannot, then, give definitions of the Church except to say that it is the blessed Body of the Divine-human Christ. It is the Body which Christ assumed from Panagia and deified it, and the Saints become members of this Body. Christ used other images to express it, such as the image of marriage, of bridegroom and bride, the vine, etc., while the image of the body was used by the Apostle Paul. And it can be said with certainty that this is God's revelation to the Apostle Paul. As Saul was journeying to Damascus to arrest the Christians, Christ appeared and said to Him: "Saul, Saul, why are you persecuting me?" While Saul was persecuting the Christians, Christ took the persecution upon Himself. It was in this way, as indeed also from other occasions, that the Apostle Paul came to use this image.

Father George Florovsky, one of the most eminent Orthodox theologians of our time, speaking of the Church, says: "It is impossible to start with a formal definition of the Church. For, strictly speaking, there is none which could claim any doctrinal authority. None can be found in the Fathers. No definition has been given by the Ecumenical Councils... One does not define what is self-evident... One has to return from the school-room to the worshipping Church and perhaps to exchange the school-dialect of theology for the pictorial and metaphorical language of Scripture. The very nature of the Church can better be described and portrayed than adequately defined... Probably even this description will be convincing only for those of the Church. The mystery is apprehended only by faith"[2].

Almost all the contemporary theologians are saying that we cannot find any definition which will fully render the content of the Church, but only that the Church is the Body of Christ, and we can use various images to characterise it. Here I would like to mention particularly John Karmiris and Panagiotis Trempelas. They confess that we cannot define the Church as the scholastic theologians of the West do. And this is because, among other things, the Church is a reality which we live and not an object which we examine.

Apart from the image of the body, which is used as much in Holy Scripture as in the patristic teaching, there are also other images which manifest this communion and union of Christians with Christ.

Speaking about the great value of the Church, St. John Chrysostom says that it is seen from the many names which it has. Christ, Who is its true Bishop, its Head, has many

---

2. George Florovsky, op. cit. p.57f

names. He is called father, way, life, light, arm, means of atonement, foundation, door, sinless, treasure, lord, God, son, only-begotten, form of God, image of God. One name is not enough for us to learn the whole. "But the countless names are in order that we may learn something about God, even if little". Whatever happens through Christ, Who is the Head of the Church, happens also through the Church, which is His Body. "Therefore the Church too is called by many names". Holy Scripture calls it a mountain, to show its firmness, it is called a virgin to indicate incorruption, queen for its sumptuousness, barren woman who gives birth to seven, to signify productiveness. There are many names in Holy Scripture to show the peculiarities and characteristic features of the Church. As Chrysostom says again, the Church "is now a bride, now a daughter, now a virgin, now a servant, now a queen, now barren, now a mountain, now a paradise, now a high yielding investment, now a lily, now a spring, she is all things". But frequently these images which are used are not bodily ones. For the mountain is not a virgin, the virgin is not a bride, the queen is not a servant on the human and bodily level, while "the Church is all things". All these images express the peculiar features of the Church.

And St. Maximos the Confessor does not define the Church, but he uses many images. Among the many expressions are the following. The Church is "an image of God", "an image of the visible and invisible essences of the existing world", "an image of the soul".

I think that in developing the subject of the Church in this section I must not overlook something which is being said today and distorts what precisely the Church is.

Many people, in speaking of the Church, mean either the hierarchy, that is only the Clergy and particularly the

Bishops, who constitute the Pastoral order in the Church, or only the laity, who have been baptised in the name of the Trinitarian God. But these views are erroneous and express Western thoughts about the Church. I think that it will be useful to have a broader analysis of this point in order to clarify some essential elements.

As we said before, the Church is the Body of the Divine-human Christ. The Christians are the real members of this Body. Thus the Church can never be an abstract organisation nor an abstract institution, but it is the unity of the Christians with Christ. But the Christians are divided into two basic categories, Clergy and laity. The distinction is not related to privileges with regard to degrees of salvation, but to what those gifted Christians who are going to help the others towards deification, i.e. the pastors who will lead the laity, should be in the Church.

So the Clergy and laity constitute the people of God. This, moreover, is not abstract, nor is the unity of Clergy and laity with Christ abstract, it is not only connected with the Sacrament of Baptism, because Baptism is not isolated from the whole life of the Church. St. Symeon the New Theologian says characteristically that the baptised and those steadfast in the faith will be saved. Moreover, Baptism is connected with the Sacrament of the Divine Eucharist. Thus, when we say that the Clergy and the laity living in Christ constitute the Church, it means that both Clergy and laymen are connected with the sacramental life of the Church, not magically, but ascetically. This means that they are connected with the purifying, illuminating and deifying energy of God.

In the patristic teaching it is clear that the three degrees of priesthood –deacon, priest and bishop– are connected with the three stages of the spiritual life, which are purifi-

cation of the heart, illumination of the nous and deification. This means that the priesthood either is a fruit of God's
purifying, illuminating and deifying energy or at least is
orientated in that direction. If it is neither the one nor the
other, then the priesthood is not taken away, there is no
deposition, but it is not satisfying its pastoral ministry. The
work of the Clergy is twofold. First, to perform the Sacraments, and second to guide the faithful towards living the
life of the Sacraments. But also, in order really to be members of the Church and to belong to the Body of Christ, the
laity must partake, or struggle to partake, of the purifying,
illuminating and deifying energy of God.

These things are being said with the understanding that
through Baptism we are enrolled as members of the Church.
However, if we do not activate the grace of Baptism by the
whole ascetic life which the Church has, then we are not
really members of it. We can make a division. It is one
thing to be a potential member of the Church, to have accepted the possibility of becoming a real member, and it is
another thing to be an active member of the Church. St.
Gregory Palamas uses the image of the son of the King.
He is born in the palace and has the possibility of becoming King, of ascending the throne. But if in the meantime
he dies, then he loses these rights. The same is true for
everybody. By his biological birth he has the possibility of
becoming heir to his father's estate. But if he dies prema-
turely or if he is expelled from the house, then he loses the
possibility of inheriting the good things. Christ says about
the bishop of Sardis: "I know your works, that you have a
name that you are alive, but you are dead". True, he can
repent, and therefore he is advised to "be watchful" and
"repent", but at that moment he was spiritually dead. This
does not mean that he did not perform the Sacraments, but

that he performed them as a dead man. Nikolas Kavasilas says: "Let us live life, attracting sanctification through the mysteries from that head and heart" until we are bound together with Christ, until we are members of Him, "flesh of his flesh and bone of his bones". However, when we become dead members, we cannot taste the life. "When we cut ourselves off and fall away from the wholeness of the All-holy body, we taste the holy mysteries in vain; for life will not pass through to the dead and cut off limbs".

Thus in the Church some are members potentially, some actually, and to express it better, some are dead limbs and others are living ones. This distinction, dead and alive, is seen in all the biblico-patristic tradition of the Church. And it is a pity when we do not know this whole tradition and teach that all who receive only Holy Baptism are members of the Church. To be sure, there are also members who have cut themselves off completely from the Church. But some dead members have the possibility of being made alive by the operation of divine grace and their own cooperation.

In this sense it is said that the Church is a spiritual clinic, a place of cure, or, as St. John Chrysostom calls it, "the great and marvellous capacious inn". And just as there are doctors, nurses and sick people in the hospital, the same is true in the Church as well. There are the doctors who know personally what is health, what is illness and the method of cure, there are nurses who help the doctors in the work of curing and there are the sick who are seeking the cure.

In the Epistles of the Apostle Paul it is seen that in the Church there are the glorified, the illuminated and the private individuals. The glorified are the deified, who partake of God's deifying energy, the illuminated are all who have noetic prayer but have not yet reached deification, and the private individuals are those baptised with water, who are in a state of purification and have not yet received the Holy Spirit. After these categories there are also those without faith who have not yet entered the stage of purification and have not yet received Baptism[3].

On these presuppositions the holy Fathers call the Church a communion of saints. It is not a collection of people who were once baptised and are in a state of stagnation, but a communion of charismatic people. Thus we can understand that the Church is life, and not a place of ideology. Within this perspective St. John of Damaskos called the Church an "orderly whole chosen by God", "the people of the saints", "Christ's people", "lambs of God, holy people". In this sense, as Father George Florovsky says, the Church is a sacred community which is clearly distinguished from the "world", that she is a holy Church. "St. Paul obviously uses the terms 'Church' and 'Saints' as coextensive and synonymous".

Therefore it is a mistake for us to regard the Church as an ideological, religious or even magic place, but we should regard it as the Body of Christ and a communion of deification. With these presuppositions we can experience in the Church Christ's victory over death. If we do not die the death and the sting of death, which is the sin in us, by the power and energy of God, if we do not change from dead to living members of the Church, we cannot feel Christ's victory over death, sin and the devil. And then for us the whole work of the divine economy will not be a personal existential fact, but simply a historical event. Therefore the Church is a place of life and not an object of thought.

---

3. John Romanides: The ancestral sin, ed. Domos, 28-29

3. The characteristics of the Church

In the Creed we confess that we believe "in one, holy, catholic and apostolic Church". Precisely these four words show us the characteristics of the Church. We shall have to look at them more analytically, because in this way we shall be able to interpret further what has previously been said about the Church.

a) One

The Church is one. There are not many Churches. It is a function of the fact that the Church is the Body of the Divine-human Christ. Christ has a Body; He cannot have many bodies. Since the Head is one, the Body is also one.

Christ said to the Apostle Peter, who confessed His divinity: "you are Peter, and on this rock I will build my church" (Matt. 16. 18). Here the word 'church' is put in the singular and not in the plural. The Apostle Paul writes: "we, being many, are one bread and one body". There are other places too which refer to this fact, but I do not want to quote them here. In any case it is seen clearly also from them that the Church of Christ is one.

In speaking of the oneness of the Church we have two basic things in view. One is that in spite of the plurality of the members, there is one body, and secondly, that it is the unique place of man's salvation.

First we must say that the Church is single in spite of the large number of its members. Christ expressed this fact by the picture of the flock and the shepherd. Since the shepherd who guides the sheep is one, and all the sheep make up one flock, it means that the unity of the Church is not abolished by the large number of the faithful, and of local

Churches, which, however, are united and bound together in their faith and life. Each local Church is not one of many so-called Churches, but the Church of Christ. Nor do the parishes break the unity of the Church, because each parish is the Church in miniature. It is about the same as it is with the lamb, the Body of Christ. At the Holy Table Christ is "broken and not divided", and therefore when we commune of the Undefiled Mysteries, we do not eat a part of Christ, but the whole Christ, because Christ "is shared inseparably in shares". Thus, in spite of the existence of many local Churches and parishes, the unity of the Church is not broken. The breaking happens through heresy. Then indeed we do not have the breaking up of the Church, but a breaking apart of the members of the Church and their withdrawal from it. The oneness of the Church is not lost, but the heretical members are broken away from this oneness, they do not belong to the united Body of Christ.

St. Maximos the Confessor says that, while the Christians are divided into categories according to age and race, nationalities, languages, places and ways of life, studies and characteristics and indeed "having been divided from one another, and most having been born into the Church different, and reborn and recreated through it in the Spirit", still it "gives equally to all and favours them with one divine form and designation, to be Christ's and to carry his name". And Basil the Great, referring to the unity of the Church, says characteristically: "The Church of Christ is one, even if it is addressed from different places". These passages and especially the life of the Church do away with every nationalistic tendency. Of course we cannot do away with the nations and the native lands but we can do away with nationalism, which is a heresy, a great danger to the Church of Christ.

The unity of the Church is internal. It emanates from its connection with Christ: first and foremost, from the common faith, which is life, from the common worship, and from the common place of man's cure. Just as the scientists of one branch use the same means and the same methods throughout the world for discovering something, the same is true in the Church. All the members use the same manner of cure. And of course in this way they show themselves to be true members of the Church.

Furthermore, the Church is the sole place of salvation. In the Church we have the assurance that we shall attain communion and unity with Christ and will become real members of Him. And in this way we can arrive at deification. Of course also outside the Church there is a chance to partake of grace, as in the Old Testament, but only in the Church can one become a member of the Body of Christ, eat the Body and drink the Blood of Christ.

Those who separate themselves from the Church do not break its unity, but they themselves, as we said before, are cut off from it and lose the possibility of being united with the Divine-human Body of Christ. Therefore St. Maximos the Confessor says: "Let us rather guard the great and first medicine of our salvation: I mean the good inheritance of the faith; confessing it boldly in soul and body as the holy Fathers taught us".

In the Church one can live all the gospel virtues. That is why without the true faith there is no true love, nor true justice and peace. Therefore the very first task of the Christian is to keep united with the Church, to have the faith both as a confession and as life in order to be able to have all the gospel virtues as well.

It is true that today there are people who speak of the union of the Churches. But this term is worthless theologically. We cannot speak of union, but of a unity of faith. We cannot speak of Churches which are separated and struggling to reach the truth and union, but about the Church which is always united with Christ and has never lost the truth, and about people who have broken away from it.

Some people who speak of union of the Churches use to satiety Christ's archpriestly prayer, which is in the Gospel according to John, and especially the point where Christ asks the Father that the disciples "may be one" and "that they all may be one" (John 17, 20-22). But if anyone reads the whole text attentively, he will discover that Christ is not referring to a union of the Churches which will come about in the future, but to the union of the Disciples which will come about on the day of Pentecost, when they will receive the Holy Spirit. This text speaks of the glorification of the Apostles which took place at Pentecost. Actually, at Pentecost the Apostles became members of the Body of Christ, they saw the glory of God, they reached deification, and so attained unity together in the single Body of Christ. Anyone who experiences Pentecost in his personal life attains this unity[4]. The Apostle Paul, although he was not present with the Apostles on the day of Pentecost, is portrayed by the Church in the icon of Pentecost, because he too reached the vision of Christ and therefore has unity with the other Apostles.

b) Holy

Since the Church is the Body of Christ, it is holy. It was sanctified and purified by Christ, who assumed it and made it His Body.

---

4. John Romanides

Referring to the holiness of the Church, the Apostle Paul says: "Christ loved the Church and gave himself for it, that he might sanctify and cleanse it with the washing of water by the word, that he might present it to himself a glorious church, not having spot or wrinkle or any such thing, but that it should be holy and without blemish" (Eph. 5, 25-27).

The Church in the Old Testament resembled a prostitute, and Christ sanctified it, made it a virgin. St. John Chrysostom analyses this truth graphically: "For the miracle of the bridegroom is that he took a prostitute and made a virgin". And then he writes that in the human biological data marriage destroys virginity, whereas "with God marriage restored virginity". Analysing this great mystery still further, Chrysostom says: "God desired a prostitute... Yes a prostitute: I mean our nature". God desires the prostitute "in order to make her a virgin". And indeed He does not send any angel, Cherubim, Seraphim or any of his servants, "He presents Himself, the lover". And since the prostitute did not want to rise high, He Himself goes down. He goes into her hut. He sees her drunk, finds her covered with wounds, enraged, pestered by the demons. He approaches her; she flees. He invites her, saying: "I am a physician". He imitates her manners. Then "he takes her, adapts himself to her", that is to say, he becomes betrothed to her, gives her the ring, that is to say the Holy Spirit.

Then Chrysostom presents a dialogue between Christ and the former prostitute. Christ says to her: "Since you were produced in Paradise, how did you fall from there?" She answers that the devil cast her out of Paradise. And Christ goes on: "You were produced in Paradise, and he cast you out; behold, I produce you in myself, I bear you". Now you no longer have a body and you have nothing to fear from the devil. The prostitute replies: "But I am a sinner and unclean. "And Christ says: "Do not worry; I am a physician". I know my own tool, I know how it was earthenware and was broken. "I shall remake it by the bath of rebirth and consign it to the fire".

I have cited these words of St. John Chrysostom, because they show what the Church is and that the Church has been sanctified by Christ. They also show that the Church is holy not through its members, but because its Head, Christ, is holy. The holiness of the Christians emanates from the holiness of Christ, it is in reality a partaker of the sanctifying grace of Christ. Thus it is not the good people that are holy, but those who partake of the deifying energy of God.

Then, since the Church is holy, so also its work is sanctifying. The aim of the Church is to sanctify its members, to guide them to illumination and deification. The sanctifying work of the Church is done through the Sacraments and the ascetic life, that is to say through its whole method of cure. Of course, not partaking of God's deifying energy is an illness. It is not a matter of a psychological condition, but of a spiritual fact. Thus, all of us who are ill make use of the true method of cure and partake of the purifying and illuminating energy of God. And in this way we too are sanctified and are true members of the Body of Christ. We stop being dead, and become living members.

c) Catholic

The term 'catholic' originates with Aristotle and means whole, entire, "the common name in contrast to that of each one". Furthermore, we can say that the term 'catholic' is identified and linked with what is Orthodox.

When we say that the Church is catholic, we mean it in three particular respects. First, that it exists in the whole world, second, that it has all the truth about God, man and man's salvation, and third, that the life which the Church has is common for all Christians, for all its members.

In the first place it is called catholic because it is in the whole world. There is no place in which the Orthodox Church does not exist. St. Kyril of Jerusalem gives this definition: "It is called catholic because it is spread throughout the world... because it is everywhere in the world from end to end of the earth... because of the unity of the Churches spread everywhere, all of which make up one catholic whole in the bond of the Holy Spirit". So then the presence of the Church in the whole world and its unity with the power and energy of the Holy Spirit characterise it as catholic.

Then it is called catholic because it has the whole truth, as it was revealed on the day of Pentecost. Here we must point out that the scholastic theology of the West teaches that through the ages we have greater deepening in the dogmas of the faith and that they are still developing further. But this is not orthodox teaching. We believe that on the day of Pentecost the Apostles reached deification, experienced Revelation and so reached the whole truth. Those who through the ages reach deification share in the same experience of revelation. But this truth is formulated and expressed in every epoch, as heresies appear. Thus we have not developed and gone deeper in the faith, but on the one hand, we struggle to live the faith, and on the other hand we are preserving the expression of faith in terms that will protect it from wrongdoings and distortions.

St. Ireneos, Bishop of Lyon, writes: "The Church, having received this message and this faith, although spread throughout the world, carefully keeps it, as living in one house: and nevertheless it trusts all, as it has one and the same heart".

In this sense catholicity is bound up with Orthodoxy. Orthodoxy preserves the whole truth, both as revealed and dogmatic, and as experience, while heresy breaks the catholicity of the truth, because it takes up one side of the truth and overlooks the other. For example, Arios did not deny that the Angel of the Lord appears in the Old Testament, but he denied the divinity of the Word. The Monophysites did not deny the divine nature, but they overemphasised it at the expense of the human nature, whereby they did away with the possibility of salvation. We observe this in all the heresies. They take one part of the truth, separate it from its catholicity, and overemphasise it at the expense of the whole. Thus the Orthodox-Catholic Church teaches, as St. Kyril of Jerusalem says, "In a catholic and complete way all the dogmas which should come into the knowledge of men".

Likewise, the Church is said to be catholic because the life which it offers belongs to all; that is to say, all Christians have the possibility of attaining deification, regardless of their way of life, their occupation and the place where they live. The Orthodox person is one believing in a catholic way, a virtuous person living in a catholic way, one who applies to his life all the commandments of Christ. As Father Justin Popovits teaches, the members of the Church "live with what is His own (Christ's), they have what is His own and they know through His own knowledge, because they think with the catholic mind of the Church, and they feel with the catholic heart of the Church, and they desire with the catholic desire of the Church, and they live with the catholic life of the Church". We are members of the Church "through living the one, holy and catholic life of the Church, through the holy and catholic faith of the Church, through the holy and catholic soul of the Church, through the holy and catholic conscience of the Church, through the holy and catholic mind of the Church, through the holy and catholic will of the Church. And thus let us have everything common and catholic, the faith, and love, and righteousness, and prayer, and fasting, and truth, and sorrow and joy and salvation and deification and godmanhood, and immortality, and eternity, and blessedness"[5].

d) Apostolic

The Church is further said to be apostolic for many reasons. First, because it has its beginning in Christ. And Christ is the Apostle and High Priest of the confession. Christ was sent by His Father to make the Church His Body and so to remain united with Him forever.

The Apostle Paul writes in his Epistle to the Hebrews: "Therefore, holy brethren, partakers of the heavenly calling, consider the apostle and high priest of our confession, Christ Jesus" (Heb. 3, 1). Here Christ is called the apostle and high priest of the confession.

Likewise, the Church is called apostolic because it is based on the foundation of the Apostles. The Apostle Paul writes to the Ephesians: "Now, therefore, you are no longer strangers and foreigners, but fellow citizens with the saints and members of the household of God, having been built on the foundation of the apostles and prophets, Jesus Christ Himself being the chief corner-stone" (Eph. 2, 19-20). The Apostles are the foundation stone of the Church, not of them-

---

5. Archim. Justinos Popovich, op. cit. p.62f

selves, but because they attained the vision of God, received the Revelation and, indeed, therefore were deified.

Furthermore, the Church is apostolic because it is also patristic. The holy Fathers give us assurance of the apostolicity of the Church. The holy Fathers are successors of the holy Apostles, not simply through the transmission of the grace of the priesthood, but because they themselves also reached the same experience of the holy Apostles. Furthermore, the apostolic succession is, on the one hand, an uninterrupted ordination and transmission of the grace of the priesthood, and on the other hand, a participation by man in the purifying, illuminating and deifying energy of God. And as a result, it is guidance of the faithful by this orthodox and true method. In the teaching of St. Gregory the Theologian, but also in the teaching of Symeon the New Theologian, it appears that the apostolic succession is participation in both the sacramental grace of the priesthood and the sanctifying grace of God[6]. But also in St. Ireneos it appears that the apostolic succession is not only a series of "teachings" and "teachers", nor only a typical series of "ordinations", but at the same time it is both a fully didactic and fully charismatic teaching[7]. This means that the apostolic succession is connected with both the Sacraments and the method of cure called 'hesychasm' and ascetic life which the Orthodox Church has, and which distinguish it clearly from other traditions and other "Churches".

St. Gregory the Theologian says that Athanasios the Great is a successor to the Evangelist Mark, in spite of the

---

6. John Romanides: Romaioi or Romioi Fathers of the Church, ed. Pournara, p. 29-31 (in Gk)

7. Hieromonk Athanasios Gievtits: Church, Orthodoxy and Eucharist in St. Ireneos. Heritage, vol. 3, part 2, p. 230, Thessaloniki July 1971

passage of so many years, according to the true faith and according to the true way.

Thus the holy Fathers feel the unity within the Church. They had a common teaching and a common mind. St. Maximos writes: "I do not say anything entirely my own. What was taught by all the Fathers, I say". What "was taught" is not known only by teaching, but also through rebirth. The saints are called Fathers primarily because they gave rebirth to spiritual children and brought them life and sanctity. The same is written by St. John of Damaskos: "We accept all those things which have been handed down by the Law and the Prophets and the Apostles and the Evangelists. We know and revere them, and over and above these things we seek nothing else". And then he says: "Let us be content with these things and let us abide in them, and let us not step over the ancient bounds or pass beyond the divine tradition".

There is no difference in the holy Fathers as to the teaching, nor as to the method of the cure of man. All the holy Fathers have a common mind and a common life. They bequeath the same method of cure, the same way to cure man and, of course, they have arrived at the same results. When there is anyone who differs in his teaching and ascetic way of life, it means that he is not a successor of the holy Apostles. He may have an outward succession, but not also the inner side of the Apostolic succession.

To be sure, some people maintain that even in the holy Fathers there is still a difference in dogmatic matters as well. But this is not true. He who examines things superficially sees differences. Those who maintain something of the sort are using such examples as the phrase of St. Kyril of Alexandria "one nature of the Word made flesh", about which some people say that it was influenced by the monophysites. However, anyone who examines carefully the teaching of St. Kyril will be convinced that there is no difference in the essence of the matter. St. Kyril uses the terms 'nature' and 'hypostasis' as equivalents, because in Alexandrian theology nature was connected with the hypostasis, while in Cappadocian theology nature was connected with the essence. This difference is verbal, it is a matter of terminology. In reality St. Kyril is very orthodox. This is seen also from another example. In the Creed of the First Ecumenical Council it is seen that the essence is identified with the hypostasis, while in the Second Ecumenical Council, without its being seen that we have a revision of the First, the essence was separated from the hypostasis. No one can say that the Fathers of the Second Ecumenical Council, and especially the Cappadocians, changed the teaching of the champion of Orthodoxy, Athanasios the Great. Thus through the ages we can have a development in terminology, but never in the Revelation and in the way and method of sanctification.

The view which prevails today –that we need to change our terminology, to transfer the content of the Revelation to new terms and to our own verbal schemes and is characterised as neopatristic theology– is dangerous. And this is because if there is a case for making some changes, it must be made by Fathers of the Church, who are living also today, and all of them have the ascetic method and live fully the hesychastic way of life which is presupposed by the dogmas of the Church. Usually those who wish to make some changes are characterised by a superficiality which can be seen in that they do not experience the traditional method of cure. These men do not know, they overlook and oppose hesychasm, which is essentially the stages of spiritual perfection, that is to say purification, illumination and deification. And this creates the danger. Besides, all the heretics attempt to form new terms, being released from the whole hesychastic tradition of the Church. Heresy is distinguished by the way of life and, as a result, by the way of theologising, or of course the other way around. Usually these things go together.

In order to finish the subject, I can say that the Church is Christ's Body and a communion of deification. The characteristics of the Church are: "one, holy, catholic and apostolic", and they are not independent of one another. Each presupposes the other.

The Church is not a human organisation, it is not a list of dead people. It is the Divine-human Organism. And we must constantly struggle to be and to remain living members of the Church, to experience, not intellectually but spiritually, the unity, catholicity and apostolicity of the Church.

3

Orthodoxy,
according to the holy Fathers

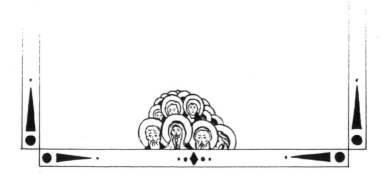

Orthodoxy,
according to the holy Fathers

In the preceding chapter we saw analytically that the Church, as we confess in the Creed, is one, holy, catholic and apostolic. Interpreting these characteristics of the Church we have said that "one" refers to the one Body of Christ; "holy" refers to the fact that it has been sanctified by its head, which is holy; "catholic" refers to the fact that it contains the whole truth, which is identified with being worldwide and Orthodox; and "apostolic" refers to the fact that it rests on the foundation of the holy Apostles and the holy Fathers, who are their successors in nature and essence.

These four characteristics of the Church converge in the fact that the Church is linked and identified with Orthodoxy. Therefore in speaking of Orthodoxy we connect it with the Church and in speaking of the Church we connect it with Orthodoxy, so we speak of the Orthodox Church. This is very basic, because Orthodoxy estranged from the Church becomes a simple ideology, and the Church, cut off from Orthodoxy, becomes simply a human administrative organisation.

In the present chapter we shall undertake to see more

analytically that the one, holy, catholic and apostolic Church
is the Orthodox. And this, of course, will be on the basis of
the teaching of the holy Fathers. Concretely, at first we
shall look at just what the word Orthodoxy means, what
Orthodoxy is, and then we shall look at the teaching of
some holy Fathers about the fact that the one Church is
identified with Orthodoxy.

What is being said may seem a little tiring and theoretical. I shall try to simplify it and make it concrete, as far as
possible, of course. Nevertheless it has to be said, because
the dogma is connected with the ethos of the Church and
the truth of the faith is closely connected with life. The
dogma is not an abstract philosophy, and life, ethos, is not
a practical occupation with something, but dogma and ethos
are interpenetrating. And of course this means that distortion of the dogma has direct results in distorting the ethos,
just as distortion of the ethos also involves distortion of
the dogma.

It is necessary for these matters to be emphasised, because everyone today is talking about acquiring a way of
life. We say that Christianity is a way and attitude of life.
This, of course, is correct with certain presuppositions. But
of course there is the justified objection that all the human
systems speak of a way and attitude of life. In the Church
the way and attitude of life is clearly very different, because it is connected with the Revelation of God, which is
expressed through the dogmas and terms of the Church.
And it is important for us to know the dogmas of the Church,
because they show us the precise course of navigation and
the precise way to go. The dogmas are the medicines which
cure man, so that when he sees God at the Second Coming, this sight will be light and not fire, will be Paradise
and not Hell.

Since many Christians do not know the dogmas of the Church, they very easily seek their salvation in other areas as well, ending by going to sorcerers in order to find the solution to some problem which is bothering them. So elaborations of such topics are essential and very useful.

1. The term 'Orthodoxy'

Very often we use the term 'Orthodoxy' which, as I said before, we should associate with the Church. We shall look at this more analytically later on. Here we must chiefly analyse what this term means.

The word 'Orthodoxy' is made up of two words, which together mean 'right glorification' or 'right doctrine'. 'Doxa' has the two meanings of 'belief', the opinion which we have about a subject, and 'glorification'. These two meanings go together and are mutually complementary. So Orthodoxy means the true, correct faith and the true glorification of God.

This combination suggests to us the truth that a true faith leads to the true glorification of the Trinitarian God. If the faith about God is erroneous, then the glorification of God will be erroneous. If, for example, we believe that God is a higher power which directs the world and not the personal Trinitarian God, then also the worship will refer to that abstract God, and will not be personal and true.

The true faith cures man and so guides him to the real worship of God and true communion with Him. Therefore the trueness of the faith is seen from the trueness of the cure of the person. If a faith does not cure man, it is not true. On this point we can maintain that Orthodoxy, as to method, resembles the sciences of today. A theoretical truth of science is confirmed by its results. Thus the faith of the

Church, Orthodoxy, has results, it can cure man. And I believe that on this point the difference between the Orthodox Church and other "Churches" is clearly visible. The orthodox faith recognises the real illness of man, pinpoints it effectively, recognises clearly what is real health, which is deification, but also recognises well the methods by which it will cure the sick man. These essential presuppositions determine the genuineness of the faith. If we examine carefully all the dogmatic differences between the Churches, that is to say, between Orthodoxy and the other "Churches", we shall see that in reality they are made explicit on the matter of knowing the illness and the method of cure.

The true faith is God's Revelation to man and not man's discovery. And indeed God revealed the whole truth about Himself and the salvation of man not to men at random, but to the saints, who were worthy of receiving this Revelation, because in reality the Revelation is not independent of the deification of man and the vision of God.

The saints handed down this Revelation, which the Apostle Paul called "ineffable words", to their disciples in order that they might be reborn into the life in Christ. The Apostle Paul writing to the Corinthians says: "For I delivered to you first of all that which I also received" (1 Cor. 15, 3). Thus they received the Revelation and the tradition. This tradition of the faith was not simply teachings, but mysteries. The Corinthians were given rebirth by the Apostle Paul, that is why he himself had the courage to invoke his paternity. He writes characteristically: "For though you might have ten thousand instructors in Christ, yet you do not have many fathers; for in Christ Jesus I have begotten you through the gospel" (1 Cor. 4, 15). Here is the clear distinction between instructors in Christ and fathers who beget spiritual children through the gospel.

The former teach outwardly and theoretically, while the latter beget spiritually through the Tradition and by guiding people to the experience of the Revelation. And of course the Apostle Paul regards himself as the father of the Corinthians, and with this presupposition he reproaches and advises them.

Thus the orthodox faith is closely linked with receiving the Revelation, that is to say with the experience and transmission of it, with the struggle for men's cure so that they may attain the experience of the Revelation. This orthodox faith is also expressed in the dogmas, which are in reality boundaries, boundaries of life and death, boundaries which distinguish the cure from the illness, the true cure of man from the false one.

Consequently, the orthodox faith is linked with the Orthodox Tradition, because what the saints receive they hand down, and this remains in the Church. Whether we say 'orthodox faith' or 'Orthodox Tradition', it is the same thing. And of course it is not abstract speculation, it is not an abstract life mingled with sentiments, fine words and aesthetics, but it is man's cure so that he may reach God. The saints were cured and attained the experience of Pentecost, and then they cured their spiritual children so that they too might reach Pentecost, that is to say, they might reach deification, the likeness[1].

At this opportunity I want to stress a point which is important in my opinion. Influenced by Western manuals, we often say that the sources of our faith are two, Holy Scripture and the Holy Tradition. Without completely excluding this position, I should like to make clear that the

---

1. See further analysis in Archbishop Sinai, Pharan, and Raith Damian: Orthodoxy and Tradition, "Ecclesiastic Truth", no. 85/16.4.1980

source of our Faith is one. And this is Pentecost, the Revelation, which happened once in history and, after that, everyone is given the possibility of experiencing it in his personal life. Pentecost is the highest point of Revelation. The saints attain the experience of Pentecost, that is to say the experience of deification, of partaking of the deifying energy of God. Afterwards this experience, which is the so-called "uncreated words", is conveyed through created words and conceptions, that is to say, through Holy Scripture and the Holy Tradition. Within this perspective we can examine the interpretation of Holy Scripture and the patristic works. When we are disconnected from the atmosphere of the Church, it is completely impossible for us to interpret Holy Scripture and the patristic texts, as well as the decisions of the Local and Ecumenical Councils. We have absolute respect for Holy Scripture and the works of the Fathers, as well as for the decisions of the Ecumenical Councils, because they are written expressions of the Revelation.

At all events, Orthodoxy is connected and identified with the right faith and the right tradition. And of course both the right faith and the right tradition are closely connected with true worship and the true cure of man. Faith, tradition, worship and cure are indissolubly bound together. Their unity is such that it is impossible for anyone to live in an orthodox way when disconnected from one of these realities. It is only within this framework that we can speak of Orthodoxy.

2. Orthodoxy according to the holy Fathers

The subject is very great and I shall not refer to all the patristic witnesses. I shall mention some representative voices: the teaching of St. Gregory Palamas, St. Maximos the Confessor, St. Ireneos, Bishop of Lyons, and Nikolas Kavasilas. And of course we shall not look analytically and fully even at the teaching of these saints about the subject which concerns us, but at some suggestive witnesses. However, the things observed will be expressive and characteristic.

a) The truth, according to St. Gregory Palamas

St. Gregory Palamas is a great Father of the Church. He lived in a difficult time for the Church, in a time of danger of secularisation of the truth of the Church, of the true faith. The fact that he struggled both to protect orthodox theology on the subject of the essence and energy of God, and for hesychasm, the method of curing man, shows that the theology of the Church is intimately connected with the ascetic life. Distortion of the theology about the essence and energy of God and distortion of the way of asceticism, which constitutes what is called hesychasm, lead man to agnosticism and pantheism.

The teaching of St. Gregory Palamas is very timely now, because the habits of life which prevail today among many Christians are animated by Barlaam's anti-hesychastic arguments, which were centred on logic, aesthetics and moralising. Therefore the teaching of St. Gregory Palamas, which is the teaching of the Church, must be given prominence today.

The philosopher Barlaam maintained that the truth is

single and was given to mankind by God, through both the philosophers and the Prophets. And he even went so far as to maintain that the experience of the philosophers was superior to that of the Prophets and Apostles. St. Gregory Palamas made the clear distinction between the two wisdoms and the two knowledges. There is human wisdom and the wisdom of God. The wisdom of God is revealed to the saints, irrespective of their cognitive power. Even the most illiterate can reach participation in the deifying energy of God. Thus the truth is a revelation of God to man, a manifestation.

St. Gregory Palamas maintains in an orthodox way that the truth is identified absolutely with the Church. He writes characteristically: "those who are of the Church of Christ are of the truth; and those who are not of the truth are also not of the Church of Christ". The Revelation of God and man's partaking of the deifying grace of God are equally true. And this truth is identified and linked with the Church. Whoever, then, falls out of the real experience of truth, whoever severs his link with the truth, also falls away from the Church.

This position appears in many texts of St. Gregory Palamas. I would like here to mention a confessional text of the saint, in which among other things the following things are said: "Let us accept all the traditions of the Church, written and unwritten, and above all, the most mystical and all-holy rite and communion and gathering", which is to say the Divine Eucharist, through which we are granted the communion of the Body and Blood of Christ. And then he says: "All those who do not confess and believe that the holy spirit foretold by the prophets, that the lord decreed plainly to us in the flesh, that the apostles announced that they were sent by him, that our fathers and their successors taught us, but instead have either themselves initiated heresy or continually followed those who have wrongly initiated heresy, all those we reject and subject to anathema".

This apocalyptic text appears to be the same as the Revelation which was given by Christ, by the Holy Spirit, to the Prophets, the Apostles and the Fathers. The Apostles are not set apart from the Apostles and the Fathers. Likewise it seems that those who lose this Tradition, who do not accept this revealed experience, but try by their own conjectures to create other traditions, are expelled by the Church, and of course are characterised as heretics.

In other texts St. Gregory Palamas defines devotion as being unquestioning of the teaching of the god-bearing Fathers. He writes: "So then this is true devotion, not to doubt the god-bearing Fathers", because the theologies of the saints "are a definition and mark of true devotion". This should be linked with what is called the Synodikon of Orthodoxy, that we must harmonise ourselves with "the theologies of the holy God-bearers and the devout mind of the Church".

Taking the example of the mother who chews hard food and then gives it to her baby to eat –the fluid in the mouths of mothers is nourishment for the children– he says that the holy Fathers soften the word of the Gospel with the right mouths, and so the conceptions in the hearts of the god-bearing Fathers come to offer nourishment to those who listen and obey. By contrast, the mouths of the cunning men of erroneous belief, the heretics, are full of poison and in their attempt to chew the food and offer it, that is to say, in their attempt to interpret Holy Scripture, the words of eternal life, "they become poisonous also to those who imprudently listen".

Indeed St. Gregory Palamas goes so far as to say that if

anyone believes in Christ and has been baptised, but then is unfaithful and cuts his link with Christ, he returns to the state of an unbeliever. This links with St. Gregory's theology, according to which God, by creating man, becomes his creator, by Baptism becomes his father and by divine Communion becomes his mother who nourishes him and gives him life. For anyone, then, who loses his faith and cuts himself off from his connection with Christ, since he corrupts the truth of the Church, God ceases to be his mother and father and becomes simply the creator, who brought him into existence through biological birth.

The fact that he goes back to the class of the unbeliever is connected with another dreadful saying of St. Gregory, that the heretic, one who has differentiated himself from the theology and life of the Church, i.e. Orthodoxy, is godless. Speaking of the three forms of godlessness, he says: "a second kind of godlessness is the heretics' multifarious and multiform deceit". Speaking of Sabellios and the other heretics, such as Areios, Eunomios and Makedonios and all those of like mind, he says: "all these and such men are by no means guilty of godlessness". Godlessness is ignorance of God, the worship of a different God from the one who has been revealed to us. And because heresy consists of this ignorance and it can never lead man to the true knowledge of God and since heresy worships another God, that is why it is called godless, and moreover, the heretics too are called atheists.

With these things in view, St. Gregory Palamas struggled against the heretics of his time and underwent all sorts of difficulties and persecutions. He himself confesses emphatically: "So let there be a tempter, let there be a torturer, let the fire burn, let the sword touch, let the claws be sharpened; even if every torture is moved against me, I accept it with willingness; I will wait for the information without moving, sustained by this Spirit". And these things are said by the Saint because he knows that when we alter the Tradition of the Church, when the orthodox faith is corrupted, we destroy the possibility of our cure and salvation.

So then, according to St. Gregory Palamas, the truth is identified and closely connected with the Church. Orthodoxy is the true faith and the real Church, because in it the salvation of man is made sure.

b) The right faith, according to St. Maximos the Confessor

Again we must point out that the saints are not philosophers and theoretical teachers, and therefore we cannot separate the saints into different categories and much less can we imply that they have their own authentications of the orthodox life. The saints lived the life of the Church, reached Pentecost and thus express the life of the Church. In this sense we can speak of the teaching of St. Maximos about right faith.

We said in the beginning that Orthodoxy means right faith. St. Maximos as well as all the Fathers of the Church teach that there is simple faith, or faith from hearing, and perfect faith, or faith from seeing. Perfect faith has nothing to do with accepting rational propositions and accepting ideological principles. On the day of Pentecost the Apostles experienced the whole truth, they received the complete faith, the revelation. Then they passed it on to the others. We receive the simple or introductory faith in order to go on to the purification of our heart and to illumination, that is to say, to the cure, so that we may arrive afterwards at the faith from vision of God, which saves.

We find this position in the teaching of St. Maximos the Confessor.

First St. Maximos emphasises that perfect faith is man's unity and communion with God. Faith is "a relational power or a relationship which brings about the immediate, perfect and supranatural union of the believer with the God in whom he believes". Orthodoxy leads man in this direction. Therefore St. Maximos teaches that the end of faith is the salvation of souls. Salvation, that is to say, succeeds when a man is led from simple faith to perfect faith. Therefore he maintains that "the true revelation of that which was believed is the end of faith".

Thus he gives great importance to the keeping of the Revelation, that is to say, what we call simple or introductory faith. He who keeps his faith in Christ unharmed "has in himself collectively all the divine gifts of grace". Acknowledging the true revelation makes it possible for us to remain in the true perspective of the cure. It is not at all by chance that St. Maximos characterises true faith as the first medicine of salvation. He writes: "Let us rather preserve the great and first medicine of our salvation: I mean the fine heritage of the faith". We preserve it by confessing with our soul and body, and indeed with boldness, what our Fathers taught and handed down to us.

Modifying the teaching about Christ by accepting the teaching of the heterodox "is a betrayal", that is to say it is a betrayal of the faith and a betrayal of Christ. As we said before, this betrayal not only refers to the Revelation, the revealed truth, but also to the salvation of man. If a man has a different teaching about God and man's salvation, then he can never attain deification. Therefore, according to St. Maximos, the heretics have a tongue which resembles "a two-edged sword and a sharpened razor... they slaughter souls and consign them to a trap of hell and a pit of darkness". "Hell" and the "pit of darkness" are not independent of the darkening of the nous, which is man's real illness and is true ignorance of God.

With these things in view St. Maximos uses hard phrases and words to characterise the heretics. He calls them "criminals", "impious", "dogs" which "return to their own vomit", etc. These characterisations are not used in a moralising sense but a theological one. In any case, many of the heretics were fine men, affable and "moral" Clerics. But since they departed from the true faith of the Church, they are characterised by these names.

From the teaching of St. Maximos the Confessor it seems that those who lose the faith, i.e. Orthodoxy, also lose their unity with God, the possibility of deification, and they depart from the Church, from the real Body of Christ. Orthodoxy is the One Church which has the truth, preserves the real method of cure and can guide man to true knowledge of God, which is communion with God.

c) Church, Orthodoxy and Divine Eucharist, according to St. Ireneos

St. Ireneos is a successor of the Apostolic Fathers, and his teaching on the subjects at which we are looking has great importance. It is important not for us Orthodox, because we believe that the truth of the faith does not depend on the time –which means that the Revelation is not altered with the passage of time– but it is important for the heretics, who think that Orthodoxy has been removed far away from the simple teaching of the holy Apostles. However, the holy Fathers, while they used different terms which prevailed in their time, nevertheless remained faithful to the

Revelation, precisely because they had the same experience, they used the same method of cure, which is purification of the heart, illumination of the nous and deification.

St. Ireneos, Bishop of Lyons, lived in a difficult period for the Church, in the second half of the second century after Christ. The situation was critical, because, on the one hand, the Apostles and their successors were gone, and on the other hand, various heretics, the Gnostics, had appeared, who maintained that they had "hidden knowledge" and "hidden secrets" which they alone had received from the Apostles[2]. This constituted a great danger for the Church. St. Ireneos lived in this crucial period. He had the advantage of being a personal eye-witness of the apostolic men, since he knew St. Polycarp of Smyrna, who was a disciple of John the Evangelist. With this advantage he confronted Gnopsticism with strength and courage.

According to St. Ireneos, the Apostolic Tradition constitutes the only guarantee of the divine Revelation. This Apostolic Tradition comprises the Church and all that comes to be and exists in the Church, that is to say, the Clergy, the Bishops, the Presbyters, the right faith, the gifts of grace of the Holy Spirit, the ecclesiastical order and organisation, the genuine church gatherings for worship, and all the elements which are contained in the local apostolic Churches.

The main points which make up the genuine apostolic faith and tradition are three: the Church, Orthodoxy and the divine Eucharist. And these three are united together in such a way that to detach them from one another is to distort the apostolic tradition and the tradition of the Church in general.

---

2. See further analysis in Hieromonk Athanasios Gievtits: Church, Orthodoxy and Eucharist in St. Ireneos, Heritage, vol.3, part 2, Thessaloniki, July 1971

The Church is the Body of Christ. By His incarnation Christ made the Church His Body and therefore He gave it all the gifts of the Holy Spirit. Where the Church is, there is the Holy Spirit as well.

Orthodoxy is the right faith of the Church. And for this reason the Church and Orthodoxy are closely united. Orthodoxy is nothing other than the Church, but, as we said, Orthodoxy is the true faith of the Church. This right faith comprises the preaching of the Apostles which the Church possesses, the Creed, which is the "unalterable canon" of truth, life and salvation, and the living of the whole economy of Christ within the sphere of the Church.

The Divine Eucharist is the action of the Church. It is this which gives us the assurance that the Church is the real Body of Christ. In the divine Eucharist we partake of the Body and Blood of Christ. Likewise, in the divine Eucharist, through the prayers which are said, it is confessed that God created and maintains the world, that Christ is the Saviour of man, that man is a creature of God and that the whole man (soul-body) can be deified. St. Ireneos says: "Our faith is consistent with the Eucharist and the Eucharist confirms the faith".

Thus in the teaching of St. Ireneos it is seen that there is unity between Church, Orthodoxy and Eucharist, because the Church is not understood apart from Orthodoxy and the divine Eucharist, and Orthodoxy is not understood apart from the Church and the divine Eucharist, but neither is the divine Eucharist understood apart from the Church and Orthodoxy. Orthodoxy is the true faith of the Church, and the divine Eucharist is the true action of the Church.

A chance existence of "Church" with "Orthodoxy" without "divine Eucharist" or an existence of "Church" with "divine Eucharist" without "Orthodoxy" is "a corrupt judgement" and a "heretical school of thought". Therefore we maintain that the one Church is Orthodoxy, in which there is the true divine Eucharist.

d) The unity of the Church, according to Nikolas Kavasilas

Nikolas Kavasilas, a contemporary of St. Gregory Palamas, will help us to see the subject of Orthodoxy from another side. In his book "the life in Christ" he has interesting aspects of the subject which concerns us in this chapter. Speaking of the consecration of the holy altar, which takes place at the inauguration of the Holy Church, and linking this action with the benefit offered in the life in Christ, he presents the three basic axes of the spiritual life, which also constitute the ecclesiastical ethos of the members of the Church.

He says that the factors which make up the unity of the Church are three, and they constitute the axes of the spiritual life. One is the holy altar, the second is the Bishop and the third the saints. Among these three factors there is a wonderful unity. The holy altar is dedicated by the Bishop and indeed the Bishop places under the altar the relics of the holy Martyrs. This shows that the altar, the Bishop and the saints form the axes of the unity of the Church and the spiritual life of the members of the Church.

The altar is "the beginning from which every sacred rite proceeds" and the basis and root of all the Mysteries. It is on the altar that the bloodless rites are performed and of course the divine Eucharist which is the centre of the Christian's spiritual life. The Hierarch anoints the holy altar and "by the grace of God he knows how to carry" the chrism. Thus the chrism, which is received, apart from man, by no other part of nature than the holy altar, according to St. Dionysios the Areopagite, "ushers in Jesus". It is the hand of Christ.

The Bishop blesses and sanctifies the holy altar, because it is the mystery of the sensible presence of Christ. The clothing of the celebrant during the dedication is the white garment, because he is a type of "the altar in human form". The fact that in the ceremony of consecration the hierarch kneels down and turns the purification towards himself is a type of the fact that "God truly dwells in the soul and makes the heart an altar". It is the practice of painters to depict according to an exemplar. Architects too first sketch mentally and then with their hand. So do all craftsmen. Thus also the Hierarch becomes a type of the altar. He himself is an altar and Temple of God and therefore he dedicates the altar.

The saints' relics which are placed beneath the altar are closely connected with the dedication of the altar. The power of the altar is the holy Chrism. Then too the material which will be placed underneath had to be appropriate. This is also true of the relics of the saints. "There is nothing that is more akin to the Mysteries of Christ than the martyrs". The martyrs are related to Christ in body, spirit, and manner of death, since they underwent a martyr's death for the glory of God. That is why the relics of the martyrs, before being placed under the Holy Table, are under the holy paten, which is the place of the Lamb.

There is a relationship among these three factors. The centre is Christ. The altar is the hand of Christ, the Bishop is the mystery of the sensible presence of Christ and the saints are the members of the Body of Christ.

There is a wonderful unity among these three. An altar cannot be understood without the Bishop and the saints. A

Bishop cannot be understood apart from the altar and the divine Eucharist, the centre of the mysteries, as well, nor can the saints be understood apart from the altar and the Bishop. A disturbance of these three centres of church life does not constitute an orthodox ethos and the mind of the Church.

The Orthodox Church has the truth, because it is also supported in these three centres of the spiritual life. The heretics have scattered the unity of the Church, because some of them disregard the saints, and others undervalue the altar and, in general, the sacramental life of the Church.

But also all those Orthodox who scatter this unity show that they lack catholicity, that they are possessed by heretical views. Some partake of the Sacraments and especially of the divine Eucharist, but do not recognise the Bishops and the saints. And others love the saints, visiting all the places where there are holy relics, but disregard the Bishop and do not partake of the divine Eucharist. Such cases do not constitute an orthodox ethos.

In conclusion, we can say that according to the teaching of the holy Fathers, in so far as the Church is the Body of Christ, and it is one, it means that this Body and the one Church is the Orthodox.

It is a great honour to be Orthodox. But this honour must be translated and lived as a great responsibility. The Church has the truth, the only possibility of guiding man to deification. This honour, however, is not a hereditary right, but constitutes and presupposes a hard struggle to live it in daily life. To be a true Orthodox is connected with a cruciform life. We must have the theology of the Church, but also the life of the Church. Here the patristic saying applies: "give blood, receive spirit".

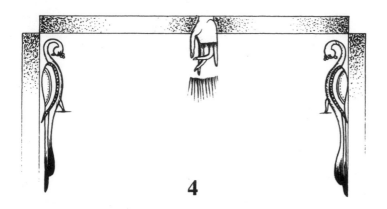

4

The Church and the Divine Eucharist according to St. Maximos the Confessor

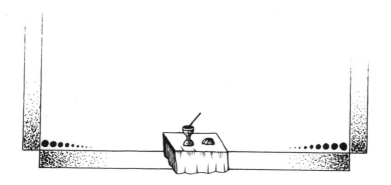

The Church and the Divine Eucharist according to St. Maximos the Confessor

When we speak of the Church and the Divine Eucharist, we cannot neglect the teaching of St. Maximos the Confessor on this subject. St. Maximos was a great Father of the Church, a hesychast and confessor, and in his life and by his life he demonstrated the close bond that there is between hesychasm and confession. From his whole teaching we know what real orthodox hesychasm is, and also what confession is. In fact, when anyone applying the methods of cure attains the knowledge of God, then he is giving the good confession and becomes a confessor of the faith and the truth.

St. Maximos's teaching about the Church and the divine Eucharist is shown clearly in an excellent and concise work of his, called "Mystagogy". In what follows we shall try to analyse some points in the "Mystagogy" of St. Maximos about the Church and the divine Eucharist. This text is rich in spiritual insights. However, we shall try to underline the most interesting ones on the subject of our concern.

1. Introductory about the "Mystagogy"

First of all it must be said that the "Mystagogy" was written at the request of a well known saint, who is called "most venerable of all". The recipient of this interpretive analysis is unknown, but we owe him gratitude for making the occasion to write this excellent and important text.

From the introduction of the "Mystagogy" it is seen that St. Maximos the Confessor was speaking orally about the Church and the divine Eucharist, analysing the mystical visions of St. Dionysios the Areopagite, on whose works he was anyway a commentator. It made an impression on the listeners, and the "most venerable of all" requested St. Maximos to write down what had been said orally, so that the text which he would send him would be "a remedy against forgetfulness and an aid for the memory".

St. Maximos hesitated at first to proceed with this work. His hesitation was due to the fact that, on the one hand, as he himself says, he was completely uninitiated in "the art of discourse", and on the other hand because he was afraid that the humbleness and cheapness of his words would insult "the sublimity and interpretation of divine things" of St. Dionysios the Areopagite, who had written about the "Ecclesiastical Hierarchies". However, he confesses that he will emphasise some of the great and lofty truths which St. Dionysios the Areopagite presents in the work to which we refer, and indeed, as he himself confesses, "such things I remember and can comprehend dimly and speak of even more dimly". He begins this work with great humility and a feeling that he cannot surpass the most holy and truly divine interpreter Dionysios the Areopagite, who, moreover, is called a blessed old man.

After that, he asks God to be a sure guide on this journey. The saint asks God to guide his thoughts as well as what he says, because God is "the sole nous of intelligent beings and intelligible things, the meaning behind those who speak and what is spoken, the life of those who live and those who receive life, who is and who becomes all for all beings, through whom everything is and becomes". About God we can use both affirmative and negative expressions, because by the first His existence is affirmed, and by the second His transcendence is shown in relation to His created works. There is no likeness between uncreated and created, between God and His creatures. The being of God is simple, unknowable and inaccessible to man and altogether impossible to interpret, because it is beyond all affirmation and negation.

In analysing the "Mystagogy" of St. Maximos it should be said that we will divide the subject into three parts. The first will be his teaching about the Church, the second, a reductive interpretation of the divine Eucharist, and the third will be a review of what has been said in this work, with corresponding exhortations. I must underline the fact that if it was difficult for St. Maximos to present the teaching of St. Dionysios the Areopagite, as he himself confesses, it is more difficult for me to set out the whole teaching of St. Maximos about the Church and the divine Eucharist. I shall mention only a few indicative points.

But before I proceed to this analysis I would like to stress in an introductory way some distinctive points from the teaching of St. Maximos the Confessor which are essential for understanding what is going to be said.

One is that the content of the "Mystagogy" is closely related to the whole theology of St. Maximos, according to which the world is created by God and therefore must aim towards Him. Because the world is not self-existent, the whole creation contains the so-called logoi of beings, that is to say, God's uncreated providential and administrative energy. By his uncreated energies God does not permit nature to pass from being to not being. Thus in the whole creation there is a movement bearing towards God. St. Maximos does not make the dialectical distinction between sensory and spiritual, which ends in diarchy and Manichaeism. When a person sees the world in this way, he changes his stand before it, he stands with respect, and yet he does not worship it. He renders thanksgiving and gratitude to God.

. The second point is that he links the Church very closely with the divine Eucharist. In any case, the fact that in his "Mystagogy" he analyses the mystery of the Church as much as the mystery of the divine Eucharist shows the importance which he ascribes to the connection between these two mysteries, and that in reality the true divine Eucharist takes place in the Church and, of course, the Church is inconceivable without the divine Eucharist.

The third point is that St. Maximos, analysing what takes place during the divine Eucharist, makes a reductive interpretation. We must say that there is a distinction between allegory and reduction. The allegorical interpretation takes its start from one passage and one fact in order to formulate another truth and reality. It functions more like an example and a type. However, the reductive interpretation mainly presents the deeper meaning of what is said - let us say also, more generally, the deeper meanings and ideas of things that are. It looks at the essence of the things that do not appear to the senses and reasoning. Thus, in the analysis of the divine Eucharist we shall see St. Maximos making a reductive interpretation, helping us to see, by comparison with the Holy Temple, another reality which escapes our bodily senses and our impure mental senses that are prone to passions.

After these explanatory points we shall come to our subject, the analysis of some teachings of St. Maximos about the Church and the divine Eucharist.

2. The Church according to St. Maximos

In speaking of the Church, St. Maximos really means, on the one hand, the union of the world and of man with God, and on the other hand, the Temple, or church building, the place where this meeting and this wonderful unity are realised. Thus the Holy Temple is interwoven with this unity, which we call the Church. This has great significance, because the Temple is also called a Church from the fact that it expresses the true Church, which is the unity of the whole world with God. From what is to be said, it will be seen that St. Maximos the Confessor takes the Temple and its whole arrangement as an example to show this unity of the world with God.

a) St. Maximos says that St. Dionysios the Areopagite regarded the holy Church as a "figure and image of God", saying that this is true in the following sense.

God created the whole world out of nothing, and He Himself maintains it personally. Therefore by His power, by His energy, "He contains, gathers, and limits" all that exists in it, "and in His providence He binds both intelligible and sensible beings to Himself and to one another". He holds both the intelligible and the sensible in a unity by His uncreated energy, while they differ from one another in nature. And therefore no beings move in discord and mutiny. God keeps them in a unity, but without any confusion and disorder.

In this sense the Church is a figure and image of God. What God does with all beings, so does the Church. While there are many members who make up the Church, and they differ in race, family, nationality, language, age, opinions, manners, occupations, knowledge, characters, dispositions, nevertheless "to all it gives and bestows in equal measure one divine form and designation, to be Christ's and to carry His name". And all the members of the Church, apart from the outward difference, have the same faith and the same life. They are called, and are, Christians. Thus, without their particular characteristics being lost, there is a wonderful unity among them.

Two examples are used to state this truth. One is the way of life of the first Church in Jerusalem, where, as is described in the Acts of the Apostles, they "were of one heart and one soul" (Acts 4, 32). The other example is the Apostle Paul's teaching that the Church is the Body of Christ, and therefore the members of the Church are members of the Body of Christ. Hence there are no distinctions and differences within the Church: "There is neither Jew nor Greek, there is neither slave nor free, there is neither male nor female: for you are all one in Christ Jesus" (Gal. 3, 28).

Thus the Church is a type and image of God, because it brings about this unity among the faithful Christians, even if there are some differences as to their characteristics, ways and places. God brings about this unity by His energy, and indeed without confusion. He is the centre of all and He creates this unconfused union.

b) With the teaching of St. Dionysios the Areopagite still in mind, he says that the Church is a type and image of the "whole universe, of the existing beings, seen and unseen". The Church is a type and image of the whole world, which is made up of invisible and visible essences, because it admits of the same union and diversity as the world.

A tangible example of this union which is experienced in the Church is the Holy Temple, the church building in which we, the members of the Church, come together to share in the Sacraments, especially the bloodless Mystagogy. The Holy Temple is one single building, but it also has its special areas. It is divided into the place called the sanctuary, which is set aside for the clergy, and the place accessible to all the faithful laity who attend, which is called the nave. Thus there are separate places for the clergy and for the faithful laity. The faithful are referred to because the catechumens do not go into the Temple proper and do not stay to the end of the Divine Liturgy.

In spite of the difference of the special places there is unity, because the Holy Temple is a single building. Furthermore, there is unity between the clergy (the Sanctuary) and the Temple proper. The Temple too is called a sanctuary, because it has the power to guide man to priesthood, to deification. But also the priesthood is called a temple because it has its source there.

This can become understandable also in the following sections. I think, however, that something can be said about it here.

The Temple proper is for the faithful, the members of the Church. The Sanctuary, and especially the altar, is for those who reach illumination and deification. There is also unity between them, because from the true faith, the true life and the true way of life one can reach deification, which is signified by the Sanctuary and the altar. Vision of God is unthinkable without action, because the vision of God, which is seeing the uncreated Light, is the entrance to action, and action is not understood if it does not have its reference and movement towards the vision of God. It is in this light that we must look at the theology of St. Maximos the Confessor about man's motion towards God. It is not a philosophical movement, but a purely theological one, which is not independent of purification, illumination and deification. We shall look at this subject below as it is analysed by St. Maximos the Confessor.

The Holy Temple, which, in spite of its division, constitutes a single reality, shows that the Church is the unity of the world. The whole world which was created by God is divided on the one hand into the intelligible world, "which is made up of noetic and incorporeal essences", and on the other hand into the sensible and bodily world, which is "ingeniously woven together of many forms and natures". In this way the entire world, the whole of creation, is in some way a Church not made with hands. The Sanctuary is the upper world and the Temple proper is the lower world, which has been given to those who live by their bodily senses.

And again we must emphasise that, according to the teaching of St. Maximos the Confessor, in spite of the difference which exists between them, the Sanctuary and the Temple proper are mutually bound together: "It shows to each other that they are both the same thing". Anyone who has the power to see perceives that the whole intelligible world "seems mystically imprinted on the whole sensible world in symbolic forms" and the sensible world exists in "all the intelligible". Analysing this point further, St. Maximos says that the sensible world is found in the mind through the logoi, through the thoughts which we have, while the intelligible world is expressed in the sensible through types and figures. However, this can be said also from the point of view that in the sensible world there are the principles of beings, God's uncreated energies. And the intelligible world becomes comprehensible through the figures.

What is said by St. Maximos is a connecting together of his whole teaching about affirmative and negative theology, about so-called natural and supranatural revelation. By the former we arrive at seeing the invisible things through the visible, while by the latter, which is realised in those who have attained the vision of God, the visible things are understood through the invisible.

Moreover, the Church is a figure and image of the world that is made up of visible and invisible essences, which have their centre in God and are directed towards Him.

c) St. Dionysios the Areopagite, as is said here by St. Maximos the Confessor, teaches that the Church is an image of "the perceptible world by itself". This is said from the following point of view. In the Holy Temple we have the Sanctuary and the Temple proper. The Sanctuary, where there is the altar, suggests heaven, while the Temple proper, which is embellished, suggests the earth. In the same way also the world suggests the Church Heaven, where God, the angels and the saints are, is the Sanctuary, and the adorned earth is the Temple proper. From this point of view we can see the so-called Church in triumph, the spiritual element of the Church, and the Church militant.

In any case, as we know from the whole theology of St. Maximos, there are no autonomised regions between the so-called spiritual and the so-called material elements. The material receives the energy and blessing of the spiritual, of the grace of God. Thus in the Church the things that are regarded as simple and not worth mentioning have great importance.

d) Following the teaching of St. Dionysios also on this point, he says that the holy Church "symbolically portrays man", but it is also portrayed "as man by him".

First of all the Church portrays man. In the Temple we see that there is a Sanctuary, with the Altar in it, and also there is the nave. Man's soul resembles the Sanctuary, the place of the priesthood. Man's nous resembles the holy Altar which is the holiest place, the centre of the soul, where the real union with God takes place. And man's body is the Temple proper. Thus with his body man practises so-called "moral philosophy", which is purification, the first stage of the spiritual life. Action in reality is linked with a person's whole ascetic effort to purify the passible part of his soul. Through his soul man experiences "natural vision", which is the inner spiritual worship, and not independent of what is called noetic prayer. And through his nous man experiences "mystical theology", the holy altar 'par excellence'.

This interpretation by St. Maximos is not unrelated to his whole theology, which comprises purification of the heart, illumination of the nous, and deification, or as they are called elsewhere, action and vision of God ('praxis kai theoria'). And from this interpretation it is seen that the Temple proper was the place for the Christians who were going through the stage of purification, the Sanctuary was for the Christians who were reaching the illumination of their nous, and the Holy Altar was for those who had reached the vision of God. The stages of priesthood which are connected with the stages of the spiritual life are not unrelated to this interpretive presentation by St. Maximos the Confessor.

Not only does the Church portray man, but man also portrays the Church and is expressed by it. By means of the body, which represents the nave, he brightens the ascetic life of his soul by observing Christ's commandments, which is done at the stage of moral philosophy. Through the soul, which resembles the Sanctuary, he offers to God "the principles of sense", purely because, that is to say, he separates them from matter, and this takes place through natural vision. At the stage of natural vision man offers the principles of things purely to God. He separates the principles of things from the passions and offers them purely to God. Through the nous, which resembles a Holy Altar, he summons within him "the silence abounding in song in the innermost recesses of the unseen and unknown utterance of divinity by another silence, rich in speech and tone". In this condition man experiences mystical theology and this means that he is deemed worthy of the indwelling of God, and he reaches the happy and blessed state of deification.

From this interpretation of St. Maximos it seems that the division of the Holy Temple shows the purpose of the Church, which is to guide the person to the holy sanctuary and the holy altar, that is to say, to natural vision of God and mystical theology, which is the illumination of the nous and corresponds to the deification of man. This is anyway the purpose of man's existence. As far as he progresses in this direction, so far also does he become a Church, a Temple of the Holy Spirit. Then he is not simply a member of the Church, but he becomes a Church. Being a member of the Church, that is, is not unrelated to being a Church. The life of the Christian is connected with a movement. And this movement, as we said before, is related to asceticism, which is linked with man's journey through purification to illumination and deification.

e) But the Church, according to St. Dionysios the Areopagite and St. Maximos the Confessor, is an image and type "of the soul considered by itself". The Church is not only an image of the whole man who is made up of soul and body, but also of the soul itself. At this point a greater analysis than the preceding position will be made. In this way we will be given the possibility of looking at the ascetic life more analytically, but also of seeing finally just who the whole man is, a living Church.

Referring to the teaching of St. Dionysios the Areopagite, he says that the soul of man consists "of noetic and vital powers". And the noetic power is moved "freely according to its will", but the vital power is moved "in accordance with nature without choice". The noetic power has the 'theoretikon', which is called nous, and the 'praktikon', which is called reason ('logos)'. The nous is that which moves the noetic power, while the logos wisely governs the vital power. The nous is called wisdom when it directs its movements altogether unswervingly towards God. Likewise the logos is called prudence, when it unites to the nous the activities of the vital power which is wisely governed by it in sensible direction. In this way, by this motion, the virtues are shared, because indeed virtue has a share in both the nous and the logos.

St. Maximos gives a more analytical interpretation of this great topic, which is connected with the salvation and deification of man.

The soul has two powers: one is the theoretikon and is called nous and the other is the praktikon and is called logos. These are the basic powers of the soul. But other powers too belong to the soul. In the noetic part, powers of the soul are in order the nous, wisdom, vision of God, knowledge and enduring knowledge, all directed to truth. In the logos part, powers of the soul are reasoning, prudence, action, virtue and faith, all directed to the good. The end of the noetic and the logos, which are the truth and the good respectively reveals God Himself. The truth points to His essence and the good points to His energy.

If we want to present this division of the soul, we will make the following schema:

Soul

Theoretiki   Praktiki

a)   nous ⟷ logos
b)   wisdom ⟷ prudence
c)   vision ⟷ action
d)   knowledge ⟷ virtue
e)   enduring knowledge ⟷ faith

Outcome of all

Truth   Good

There has to be motion of both the nous and the logos. This motion institutes the deification and salvation of man. The nous must be moved towards wisdom, because it is called wisdom when all its power is directed towards God, with the aim of reaching the vision of God, of possessing knowledge and of ending in enduring knowledge and, of course, truth. The logos must be connected with prudence, because the logos is and is called prudence, when it prudently joins the vital power which is directed by it and this means that the body too is moving towards deification. Then the prudent word advances to action, which is purification, to the acquisition of virtue and the discovery of faith. And this results in acquiring the good.

What is very important is that St. Maximos does not separate completely either nous from word or word from nous. He teaches that these things go together and that there are five unions, which revolve "around the one important union of God". The first union is the nous and the logos; the second is wisdom and prudence; the third, vision and action; the fourth, knowledge and virtue; and the fifth, enduring knowledge and faith. The whole soul of man is moved towards God and united with God with the help of the one union which manifests God, and this is the truth with the good.

This theology of St. Maximos is not mental or philosophical, but experiential. He himself, having the experience of the spiritual life, could present it in this way. No one can, by philosophical conjectures, present the teaching which St. Maximos the Confessor sets forth. The visionary power of the soul (theoretiki) is not thinking, but the nous, which moves towards the vision of God, the vision of the uncreated light, when it acquires the true knowledge of God. And the practical power of the soul is the logos which moves towards action and the acquisition of virtue. This action is nothing other than purification of the heart. St. Maximos the Confessor means that action goes along with the vision of God. And of course action is not missionary action, and vision of God is not mental conjecture about God, but action, as we said, is the effort to have a pure heart, to have all the thoughts expelled from it, while vision of God is noetic prayer and the vision of the uncreated Light.

This is important because it shows the great value of the neptic and hesychastic tradition which our Church has. And it is further important because it shows that we must not limit ourselves to outward activity, but at the same time we must proceed into the interior. Moreover, it can be said that deification is impossible to reach without the accompaniment of action.

Then St. Maximos makes a thorough analysis of how the nous moves in order to reach enduring knowledge and truth, which truth is so called because it is "infallibly known". It is a certainty that the nous is in constant motion and this motion never ceases, because God is the truth "around which the nous, moving unendingly and infallibly, never has an end to its motion, not finding a termination to which there is no distance". The nous can never stop on its journey towards God, because what has no dimensions and what cannot be understood cannot be finished. Further, the saint describes how the logos moves through prudence, to action and to knowledge. From knowledge the logos arrives at the good, where its motion stops. The motion of the nous never ceases, has no end, while the motion of the logos has an end.

When the soul, by the grace of the Holy Spirit and by its own diligence and eagerness, has been able to bring together these five unions, that is to say, when it has succeeded in uniting reason with the nous, prudence with wisdom, action with vision, virtue with knowledge and faith with enduring knowledge, without there being too little or too much of one against the other, then even the soul itself "will be united with the true and good and one and only God". Then the soul will be united with God and become by participation what God is in essence.

St. Maximos attaches great importance to this unity of the pairs, but also to the movement of the nous and reason towards the truth and the good correspondingly. There is no immobility in the spiritual life. Through the struggle which the Christian makes –strengthened, of course, by divine grace– he acquires a blessed nous, prudent wisdom, vision in action, virtuous knowledge and enduring knowledge, which is very faithful and unchangeable.

In any case, energy is also a manifestation. The manifestation of the nous is the logos, as cause, as effect of the cause. A manifestation of wisdom is prudence, of vision is action, of knowledge is virtue, of enduring knowledge is faith. From these things is created the inner relationship with truth and the good, which is God. This relationship is called divine science (that is to say perfect, sure knowledge), love and peace, and in and through them deification exists and takes place. It is called science because it offers to man, as far as possible, knowledge about God and things divine, "and a perfect embrace of the virtues". It is called knowledge, because it lays hold of the truth and offers a lasting experience of the divine. It is called love, because it shares in the full happiness of God. It is called peace, because it prepares those who are deemed worthy of this state to share in the things of God.

When the soul attains this unity, as it is described in the "Mystagogy" of St. Maximos, and is collected towards itself and God, then "there is no reason to divide it purposely into numerous things because its head is crowned by the first and only and unique Word and God". This will happen because in the Word and God, Who is creator of all beings and their principles, are all these principles, that is to say, all the words, in an incomprehensible simplicity, live and exist in the Word.

Again I must repeat, because, unfortunately, this teaching is misunderstood, that St. Maximos is not a philosopher like the philosophers who study conjecture and imagination. The logoi or principles of beings, according to St. Maximos, are God's uncreated energies, creative, governing and providential, which created the world and maintain it. Of course the logoi of beings are not self-existent, but God, through His energies, created and directs the world. Consequently the whole world contains the energies of God which give meaning to all the things that are, and which are what constitutes the deepest element of their existence. The bad thing is when we look at creation without seeing its logoi. We can say the same also about the logos in men. By this expression St. Maximos does not mean the logos which is constantly cogitated with passion, but the logos which is purified by practical philosophy and is offered pure to God. Thus when we speak of logoi we do not mean the various conjectures which come in a variety of ways and with passionate meanings. St. Maximos, therefore, is an ascetic theologian, because theology is connected with asceticism.

St. Maximos continues and says that when the soul is united with itself and God, then there will be no reason to divide it into many things by syllogisms. The soul united and gazing steadily at God, the Word of God, will itself understand the principles of beings. This means that it is only through the unity of the soul, through its purity, that the soul can see the principles of beings. So it is not a question here of an impure conjectural motion of the soul. In this way it reaches "safely both through them and harmoniously towards him". But this happens when the soul is wedded to God.

This whole analysis is presented by St. Maximos in order to relate it to the Holy Temple, because the holy Church is an image of man's soul. The things that happen in man's nous and what comes forth from it are symbolised by the clergy, that is to say the Sanctuary. The things that happen in the logos and proceed from the logos are manifested and indicated by the Nave. And these two are united and brought together in the sacrament which is performed on the divine altar. The work of the logos, which is connected with prudence, action, virtue and faith is indicated by the Nave. The work of the nous and its movement towards deification through wisdom, vision of God, knowledge and enduring knowledge is connected with the clergy, that is to say, the Sanctuary. Both movements of the soul, both nous and logos, end in deification, of which the altar is a figure. Whoever has been initiated into this mystery prudently and wisely "has been made a true Church of God, and his soul has been made divine". Thus the Church made by human hands, the Temple with its arrangement as Nave, Sanctuary and Altar, have given us a symbolic model to show us what should be our goal. Our goal is the holy altar. We should proceed from action to the vision of God, which is deification.

After this interpretation there are two further small chapters. One gives an analysis of how and in what manner the Holy Scripture is said to be a man. For just as the Church is the spiritual man and just as man is the mystical Church, so also the Holy Scripture is like man. The Old Testament is his body and the New Testament is his soul and nous. Moreover, the entire Holy Scripture, both Old and New Testaments, in its formulation with the "historical letter" is the body, while the nous of the things written and the goal towards which the nous is aiming is the soul. In the other chapter the truth is analysed about how the world is called a man and how a man is called a world.

In concluding this unit we can emphasise two basic points.

The first is that the way in which the Temple is arranged, in which the Church comes together, indicates man's journey. Outside the Temple is the place of the Catechumens and of those without faith, the unbelievers. The Nave belongs to the faithful, who are at least in the stage of purification, in the so-called moral and practical philosophy. The Sanctuary belongs to those whose nous is illuminated, who have passed to the first stage of the vision of God, which is called illumination of the nous and natural vision of God. And the divine altar belongs to those who have reached mystical theology, enduring knowledge, deification. Within this spiritual presentation we can see the necessity for the iconostases and for secret reading of prayers of the Divine Liturgy. In this light we can look at the ascetic life of the Church, which guides people from purification to illumination and deification. Liturgical life without the ascetic life does not help effectively in the regeneration of the church congregation.

The second conclusion is that a person should not simply take part in the holy ceremonies and enter the Holy Temple, but he should become a nave and a real Church. He should make his soul and body "truly a Church of God". This means making man into a Church. When a man becomes a temple of the Holy Spirit and a Church of God, then he will be able to perceive the great value of being a member of the Church.

3. The Divine Eucharist, according to St. Maximos

The things that have been mentioned thus far will be seen further within the perspective of St. Maximos's reductive analysis and interpretation of the divine Eucharist. The Eucharist, which manifests the Church as the Body of Christ, is celebrated within the Holy Temple. And the Eucharist is attended by the members of the Church. St.

Maximos with great theological penetration presents to us how one who is without faith, that is to say, who lacks the gifts of the Holy Spirit, comes into the Temple and the divine Eucharist, and how he progresses towards deification.

In his analysis St. Maximos interlaces the eschatological closely with the present: the things that will be in the future with those things which the Christian is enjoying now. Moreover, we cannot perceive the last things if we look at them apart from what God has done for man and apart from the incarnation of Christ. Thus in his whole analysis of the divine Eucharist St. Maximos presents two things. One is the work of the divine Economy, what God has done and is doing for man, and the other is the movement of man's soul, as well as of the whole man, in order to be united with God.

First we shall see that the divine Eucharist points to the whole work of the divine Economy, what God has done for man and how man is responding to this work, and what is its outcome. And then we shall see how the Eucharist signifies the soul's journey to acquiring perfection, true knowledge.

a) Divine Eucharist and Divine Economy

The divine Eucharist, as it is analysed by St. Maximos, shows Christ's great mercy towards mankind, and also how the divine Economy is experienced. All that is done and said in the Eucharist points to the stages of the journey towards deification.

The first entrance of the bishop into the Church to celebrate the Eucharist is a figure and image of the first appearance in this world of Christ in the flesh. By His work

Christ freed human nature from corruption, sin, death and the devil. These are man's greatest oppressors. Christ, who was "not liable but sinless" paid the whole debt "as under liability" and was guiding man to the original grace of the kingdom. Through His life-giving Passions He offered His salutary cure to the race of man, and thus Christ's life-giving Passions cure our own destructive passions. After entering the Nave, the bishop ascends the throne. This points to the ascension into heaven of the Great Archbishop Christ and His restoration to the supracelestial throne.

The entrance of all the laity with the bishop indicates the return of the unfaithful from ignorance and error to the knowledge of God, as well as the passage of the faithful from ignorance to virtue and knowledge. At the same time it also indicates the return of us believers from failure to do God's commandments, and by repentance, to correcting our loose and indecent way of life. The person who sins and commits passionate acts returns to virtue by his personal struggle, which is stated by his entrance into the Church.

The reading of "the holy books", the Holy Scriptures, signifies God's desires and intentions. Through what we read we receive in proportion to our capacity the counsels by which we should act. We learn the laws of the blessed struggles through which we will rightfully attain the Kingdom of God.

The spiritual enjoyment of the divine hymns signifies the delight of the divine blessings. This delight moves souls toward the clear and blessed love of God and arouses them towards hatred of sin.

The salutations of peace which are issued from within the Sanctuary on the signal of the bishop at each reading indicate that God accepts the efforts of those who fight bravely for the truth and gives peace which resolves the invisible struggles and does away with the body of sin, at the same time giving the grace of dispassion to the saints who have struggled in their battles for virtue. In this way they direct the powers of the soul to accomplishing the virtues.

After the antiphons of peace, the holy Gospel is read. It proposes to those who are zealous some suffering on behalf of the Word. Through this suffering the Word of spiritual contemplation comes to them as High Priest from heaven to constrict their fleshly understanding of the world. It restrains their earthly thoughts and, after the closing of the doors, i.e. the senses, it leads them to the vision of spiritual principles and realities. Through this so-called hesychastic movement, the return of the nous into the heart and its union with God, one becomes a son of God by grace, as will be analysed for us in what follows.

Generally speaking, the reading of the Gospel signifies the completion of the world. After the reading of the Gospel the Bishop descends from his throne and the dismissal of the Liturgy of the Catechumens takes place; the Catechumens, as well as those who are unworthy "of the divine vision of the mysteries to be displayed", leave the Temple. This passage shows that not only the Catechumens leave the Temple, but also those Christians who were not worthy of the vision of the divine Mysteries. This action indicates that the Gospel has been proclaimed to all the world and the judgement is coming. Then His holy angels will separate the faithful from the unfaithful, the righteous from the unrighteous and the saints from the sinners. A just reward will be given to each according to his life.

The closing of the doors after the departure of the Catechumens signifies the passing from material things and the entrance of those who are worthy into the spiritual world, the nuptial chamber of Christ. It also signifies the complete extinction in our senses of deceptive activity.

The entrance of the august Mysteries is the beginning and prelude of the new teaching about God's economy and the revelation of the mystery of our salvation, which is hidden in the most secret recesses of the divine.

The spiritual kiss which comes before the transformation of the Precious Gifts prefigures and portrays the concord, unanimity, and identity of views which we shall all have at the time of the revelation of the ineffable blessings to come. Moreover, the mouth is a symbol of the word. And all who commune in the Word also have communion with everything as well as with the Word, Who is the cause of every word.

The confession of the divine symbol of faith, the creed, prefigures our mystical thanksgiving in the age to come. Through it those who are granted these blessings will show gratitude to God for His great gift.

The triple exclamation of holiness proclaimed in the hymn "holy, holy, holy", represents the union and equality in honour with the bodiless powers, the angels, which will be manifested in the future. Then men's nature will be taught to sing and to glorify the single Godhead in three Persons.

The all-holy and sacred invocation of our great and blessed God, the pronouncing of the Lord's prayer, is a symbol of the personal and real adoption which is bestowed through the gift and grace of the Holy Spirit. Through this all the saints who in this life have adorned themselves with the virtues, will become sons of God and will attain adoption by grace.

The profession "One is holy, one is Lord..." which is

voiced by all the people at the end of the mystical service represents the gathering and union beyond reason and understanding which will take place between those "who have been mystically and wisely initiated by God and the mysterious oneness of the divine simplicity" in the incorruptible age of the spiritual world.

The distribution of the sacrament is participation in the divine life, and in this way men also can be called gods by grace, because they are filled with the grace of God.

The exhortation by the Bishop or Priest, "With fear of God, faith and love draw near", indicates the three classes of the saved. To the first category (with fear) belong the slaves, who do the will of God from fear. To the second category (with faith) belong the mercenaries, who out of a desire for promised benefits bear with patience the burden and heat of the day, that is, the affliction innate in and yoked to the present life by the condemnation of our first parents, and the temptations from it on behalf of virtue. And in the third category (and love) are listed the sons of God, those who are never separated from God, but struggle to maintain this relationship and unity, and they do not do it out of fear of threats or out of the desire for promised things, "but rather by the tendency and habit of soul towards what is good in spirit".

Thus, by this interpretation, the divine Eucharist indicates man's whole journey to sharing in the eternal blessings and participating in the everlasting age to come. There already exists a foretaste of the future blessings.

b) Divine Eucharist and the soul's perfection
by knowledge

The Eucharist not only points to the work of the divine Economy, in other words, to the purpose of the divine incarnation, but, in an apocalyptic way it also indicates how man is perfected and deified. It can be said that the Eucharist is a representation of the perfecting of the soul. All that has been said before applies also to the enlightened soul. This interpretive analysis shows how the divine institutions of the Church lead the soul to its perfection through true and effective knowledge.

Entering the Temple represents the distancing of the soul "from the error and confusion of external material things". The philosophers of ancient Greece, whom St. Maximos called unwise wise men said that the vision of God comes through seeing tangible things. However, the vision of God in the Orthodox Church has a different meaning and significance. It is not just the vision of tangible things, because among tangible and material things there is continual and unceasing warfare and mutual destruction. There is never a tranquil and secure situation. Through the natural vision of God, which is illumination of the nous in the theology of St. Maximos and all the holy Fathers, the soul goes inward as into a Church. This return of the soul is done with reason (logos) and by the Word (Logos), the great and true God. There it is released from all disturbance and attains deepest peace. Then it is taught the principles of beings. This is represented by the readings from the law and the prophets. The peace is linked with the divine and ardent desire for God.

This is the hesychastic movement of the soul. The nous withdraws from its dispersion among sensible and created things, enters the heart and there finds its natural condition, it aquires peace. Through this movement it passes beyond to the one and only summit, the holy Gospel, where the principles of providence and existing things meet together. Then, just as the bishop descends from his throne, so the lovers of God are granted to see with the eyes of their undistracted nous the Word and God Himself. And in this way the faithful are distinguished from the Catechumens. The Catechumens, as St. Maximos says, are those who take pleasure in sensation and are possessed by the imaginative thoughts which are connected with sensation.

Then the soul is granted to see the Word, who leads it to the spiritual understanding which is "immaterial, simple, immutable, divine, free of all form and shape". Through the spiritual kiss the soul comes to the Word of God, because it gathers "to itself" the words of salvation, and the Word teaches it through the creed to confess this with thanksgiving.

When the soul has encompassed with knowledge the principles of both tangible and intelligible things, it is led to the knowledge of revealed theology. Then the soul is taught as far as possible, one God, one essence, three Persons, unity of essence in three persons, and consubstantial trinity, "unity in trinity and trinity in unity". For the one is not divided into persons, nor are the persons combined into a unity. God remains a unity in spite of His trinity, and is a Trinity in spite of the fact that He is one. The Holy Trinity of the persons is without confusion as to essence and the holy Unity is three as to persons and mode of being. According to the characteristic words of St. Maximos the Confessor, when the purified soul is led to the experience of God, it sees one, single, undivided, unconfused, simple, undiminished, and unchangeable divinity, "completely one in essence and completely three in persons, and one single ray shining in the single form of one triple-splendoured light".

Then the soul is led to sonship by grace. And a result of this is that the soul no longer desires to belong to itself, but desires only to offer itself completely to God and to belong exclusively to Him.

Through this analysis of the divine Eucharist given by St. Maximos the Confessor, one can see the method which the Orthodox Church offers for a person to unite with God and participate in divine sonship in Christ, the participation of deification. The soul is concentrated, freed from the mastery of the senses, it is brought together into itself, the nous is illuminated and sees the principles of beings, as a result rises to the vision of God and there recognises the Trinitarian God, sees, as far as possible, the Holy Trinity - of course not the pure essence, but its uncreated energy. Orthodox theology is therefore connected with asceticism, with what is called the hesychastic method. By this method the soul is perfected and experiences the mystical divine Eucharist.

4. Recapitulation and exhortations

At the end of the "Mystagogy" St. Maximos makes a recapitulation of what he has said, which he combines with various exhortations for Christians to enter the Holy Temple and take part in the divine Eucharist.

Referring to St. Dionysios, he writes that he has exhorted the faithful to frequent and remain in the Church, the Holy Temple, and not to abandon the holy services going on in the Church. Indeed he said that the angels enroll those who enter the Temple, make them manifest to God and pray for them. Also in the Temple, especially during the holy Service, there is the grace of the Holy Spirit, which transforms each one according to his condition and leads him to those things which the holy mysteries symbolise.

Actually, in the church, especially during the divine Eucharist, the soul of the Christian is being changed. At the first entrance it is seen that unfaithfulness is expelled, faith increases, evil decreases, virtue increases, ignorance disappears and knowledge increases. The hearing of the divine words leads to permanent and unchanging habits and dispositions of faith, virtue and knowledge. The hymns signify the soul's assent to the virtues and the spiritual and noetic pleasure which come from them. The reading of the holy Gospel signifies the end of the carnal, <u>earthly</u> mind. The closing of the doors manifests the soul's desire to journey from the perishable to the intelligible world. It closes the senses and purifies them of the idols of sin. The entrance into the holy Mysteries indicates the perfect and new teaching and knowledge which God's economy offers. The kiss manifests the concord and oneness and love of each one of the faithful with himself, the others and God. The Creed signifies our gratitude for salvation. The thrice-holy manifests union and equality with the angels. The Lord's prayer signifies our adoption by grace. The "one is holy..." signifies the grace which unites us with God. The communion of the Holy Gifts shows that man has been granted to become God by grace.

The sharing of Divine grace and our adoption by grace is essential because, as St. Maximos says, what gifts man receives from the present life through the faith which is in grace he will also truly receive in the coming life.

And after this analysis the saint exhorts us never to leave

the Holy Temple, especially during the Holy Synaxis, that is to say, the celebration of the bloodless Mysteries.

5. Conclusions

The "Mystagogy" of St. Maximos the Confessor is 'par excellence' a theological, ecclesiological, mystagogical and ascetic text. It is, we could say, a summary of the whole teaching of the Church about deification. I would like to conclude by making the following points.

a) The Church, which is the Body of Christ, is associated with the church building, which itself is called a Church, and it is also associated with the divine Eucharist, which is the deepest expression of the Church. In the church building and the divine Eucharist we have living experience of the unity of the Church.

b) The structure of the church building points to the soul's journey to deification. Outside the building are those without faith, those who have not received the faith from revelation, they have not become members of the Church. We use the word 'unfaithful' in this sense. Those who are baptised enter the Temple, and the Catechumens as well, up to a point. And I can add that not just the baptised enter, but all who are struggling to be purified of passions, to be freed from their slavery to the senses, which in reality is the condition of the catechumens. Therefore all who enter are in the stage of practical philosophy. Those who are in the stage of natural contemplation, whose nous has been purified and illuminated, enter the Sanctuary. And all who have reached the vision of God are associated with the altar.

c) The whole structure of the Eucharist shows this reality. It manifests to us just what is the work of the divine

Economy. It signifies the eschatological condition of the world and of the righteous, which of course is beginning now. Moreover, through St. Maximos's interpretation of the perfecting of the soul and the acquisition of saving knowledge, with reference to the structure of the divine Eucharist, we can see the link between eschatology and the experience of divine grace in the present life.

d) The experience of divine grace through the sacraments is not independent of the ascetic life. Sacraments and asceticism are connected and cannot be understood apart from each other. The sacramental regeneration which is taking place in our time must be accompanied by and associated with bringing asceticism to the fore and assisting people through the stages of the spiritual life, which are purification of the heart, illumination of the nous and deification.

The "Mystagogy" of St. Maximos initiates us into the holy of holies of orthodox theology. Then we are real and living members of the Church of Christ.

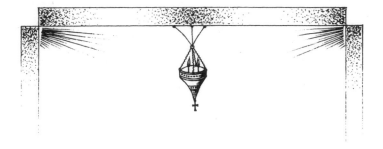

5

The mind of the Orthodox Church

The mind of the Orthodox Church

At times it is said that we ought to be characterised by having the mind of the orthodox Church. Of course this is basic and essential, because it is what makes one a real, genuine Christian.

The point is that we make several divisions in the spiritual life, and we even discriminate between Christians. We identify the genuine mind of the Church with one category of people and we exclude another. For example, we think that if we become Clergymen or monks we automatically acquire the mind of the Church; we think that we are churchmen and that the others are not. But things are not like that. And we cannot simplify these great matters in this way.

With the thoughts that are to follow we shall try to look at this subject in its true and real dimensions. We shall see what the "mind of the orthodox church" means, and then what are its characteristics.

1. Analysis of the term "mind of the Orthodox Church"

First we shall have to make a rather broad analysis of these words, because it will help us to enter more deeply into our subject.

If we open the dictionary to the word 'phronima' ("mind") we shall see that it means thought, mind, desire, knowledge, ideology, etc.

In the Biblico-patristic Tradition, however, 'phronima' is something deeper. It is not complete at the surface, but it proceeds into the depth. It indicates the whole atmosphere which distinguishes a man, his particular way of life, and furthermore, the stand which he takes on various topics.

Of the places in Holy Scripture which refer to 'phronima' I shall mention one from an epistle of the Apostle Paul. He writes to the Romans: "those who live according to the flesh set their minds on the things of the flesh, but those who live according to the Spirit, the things of the Spirit. For to be carnally minded is death, but to be spiritually minded is life and peace. For the carnal mind is enmity against God" (Rom. 8, 5-7).

We should place this passage in the whole Biblico-patristic Tradition, according to which flesh and spirit are not simply the body and soul, but something deeper. A real man is one who has body, soul and spirit, that is to say, divine grace. It is not a matter of a synthesis of the three. Man is made up of body and soul, which is to say he is disynthetic. However, just as the soul is the life of the body, so also the grace of God, the Spirit, is the soul of the soul. Consequently, according to the patristic teaching, a genuine man is one whose noetic energy is blessed by the grace of God and is turned towards God. In this sense a spiritual man is one who has in him the spirit of God, the grace of God. He is a real son of God by grace, and so experiences sonship by grace.

In the same epistle and the same chapter which develops this theme, the Apostle writes: "For as many as are led by the Spirit of God, these are sons of God" (Rom. 8, 14). Anyone who has the Spirit of God in him, which means that his noetic energy functions physiologically and is moved in accordance with nature, has noetic prayer and is a son of God by grace. By the Spirit we acquire sonship, and therefore the Apostle writes: "by whom we cry out, 'Abba Father'" (Rom. 8, 15). This cry is not different from the noetic prayer which takes place in the heart. And of course these men belong to Christ, are members of the Body of Christ, and of course members in fact of the Church. What the Apostle Paul says is characteristic: "If anyone does not have the Spirit of Christ, he is not his" (Rom. 8,9).

Therefore a spiritual man is one who has the Holy Spirit within him, not in an abstract and conjectural way, but in fact through noetic prayer. The man who does not have the Holy Spirit, even if he is baptised, even if he has virtues, is carnal. Carnality, according to the teaching of the Apostle Paul, does not refer to a category of sins, so-called bodily sins, but to the whole life of the man who is not inspired by the Holy Spirit.

The mind of the spirit, therefore, is the whole atmosphere, the whole way of life which is inspired by the Holy Spirit. And the mind of flesh is the whole way of life of the man who is not inspired by the Holy Spirit. According to the interpretation of Theophylaktos of Bulgaria, the Apostle Paul calls the mind of the flesh "men's earthly nous" and he calls the mind of the Spirit "the mind and nous which mind the things of the Spirit". The former is death of the soul, the latter is life and peace.

The mind of flesh is connected with all the passions, with the actions of the soul which move against nature. Basil the Great says characteristically: the passions grow "out of the mind of the flesh". St. John Chrysostom, interpreting the passages of St. Paul's epistle to the Romans which we mentioned above, writes: "I say that here the mind of flesh is that which is earthly, gross, after the things of this life and its wicked doings". And furthermore, the holy Chrysostom observes: "a mind of flesh is sensuality, squandering. A mind of the flesh is greed and all sin".

From all these things it seems that the word 'phronima' in the biblico-patristic Tradition means the whole turn of mind which prevails in a man from the way in which he lives, and from the relationship which he has with God. And literally, if the nous is darkened, then the whole mind is carnal. But if the nous is illuminated, which means that it has the Holy Spirit within it, then the whole mind is a mind of spirit and, of course, a mind of the Church.

Having seen what 'phronima' (mind) means, we must next look at what "orthodox" mind means.

When we speak of having an orthodox mind we mean chiefly that our nous is the nous of Christ, as the Apostle Paul says, or at least that we accept the experience of the saints and have communion with them. This is the way of life of the Orthodox Tradition and the way of life of Christ's life. The orthodox mind is expressed by the dogmas of the Church, because, on the one hand, the dogmas express the life which the Church has and the revelation which the saints have received, and on the other hand, they lead the passionate people and the babes in Christ to unity and communion with God.

We must say at this point that the theology of the Church is ascetic, that is to say, it defines the methods of cure in order for man to attain deification. Dogmatic theology is polemic, which means that it has been created mostly to oppose the heretics who have appeared and distorted the theology of the Church, with direct consequences for man's salvation. The terms 'essence', 'hypostasis', 'nature', etc., have been created to oppose the heretics. So the dogmas express the revelation and the life which the Church has and they also cure man and lead him towards deification. They are spiritual road signs. In this sense we can say that the dogmas save man and sanctify him. This happens because they cure him and give him the right orientation on his way towards God.

In His high-priestly prayer Christ says, among other things: "Sanctify them by your truth. Your word is truth" (John 17,17). St. John Chrysostom, interpreting this passage, says: "Make them holy by the gift of the Spirit, and of right doctrines... for right doctrines asserted concerning God sanctify the soul".

Of course when we speak of dogmas, we mean all the decisions of the Local and Ecumenical Councils which refer to subjects of dogma, such as Christ's consubstantiality with the Father, the divinity of the Holy Spirit, the ever-virginity of the Mother of God, the oneness of the two natures of Christ, etc. Likewise in the more general sense dogmas are all the spiritual laws which express the genuine life in Christ and lead man to attain this life. And we may recall Basil the Great's saying that all of Christ's commandments are commandments of salvation.

It is characteristic that not only those are called heretics who deny some dogmatic definition of the Ecumenical Councils, but also those who deny the words of revelation which lead man to salvation. St. Symeon the New Theologian gives us such an example.

In his time there were men who denied some of Christ's teachings, such as that about spiritual mourning - "Blessed are they that mourn" - and who also doubted the existence of holy men who had reached the vision of God and had the same grace as the Apostles and saints. St. Symeon writes: "Those whom I call heretics are those who say that there is no one in our times and in our midst who is able to keep the Gospel commandments and become like the Holy Fathers". These men "have not fallen into one particular heresy, but rather into all of them". "He who makes such a claim subverts all the divine Scriptures". And since Christ opens heaven by His commandments, "they shut heaven" by their denial of the commandments. Those who claim that it is not possible for anyone today to weep and it is impossible to apply Christ's commandment about spiritual mourning are insensitive, and they utter "defiled words against the Most High God and make the sheep of Christ a prey for wild beasts, those sheep for whom the only-begotten Son of God shed His blood".

Therefore it seems that the orthodox mind is to accept all the commandments of Christ and to live by them, because the commandments and doctrines sanctify man, that is to say, they heal him, they are the medicines which help him to get rid of spiritual blindness, darkening of the nous.

But the orthodox mind is the mind "of the Church". This means that Orthodoxy cannot be understood apart from the Church, nor the Church apart from Orthodoxy. The Church is the real and sanctified Body of Christ. Orthodoxy is the teaching of the Church and the divine Eucharist is the true action of the Church. Thus Orthodoxy, Church and Eucharist are joined together.

The whole orthodox teaching, the whole revelation is experienced in the Church. Therefore the orthodox mind is connected with the mind of the church and is unified. We cannot, then, make fragmentations of the teaching, ethos, life and order. A person expresses his mind of the Church not only by his obedience to the Bishop, but also by his obedience to the whole Tradition of the Church. As Nikolas Kavasilas has analysed it, the Bishop is closely connected with the altar and the saints. The holy Temple is sanctified and consecrated by the Bishop, who places holy relics in the altar. Hence, the centres and axes of the spiritual life are three: Bishop, Altar and saints. A denial of one of these and acceptance of the others does not constitute a mind of the Church. Moreover, just as the Church cannot be understood apart from the Bishop, the Bishop cannot be understood apart from the Church, apart from the whole Tradition of the Church.

One can maintain that anyone has the mind of the Church who accepts the Bishops and is directed by them, and at the same time accepts the Tradition of the Church. Anyone who accepts the Tradition of the Church and denies the canonical Bishops, or anyone else who accepts the Bishops and denies the whole Tradition of the Church does not have the mind of the Church.

Next we shall attempt to look more analytically at the real characteristics of the orthodox mind of the Church. It will be a spiritual mirror in which we should often look at ourselves to see whether we have the genuine orthodox mind of the Church and if not, to do everything to attain it.

2. Characteristics of the orthodox mind
of the Church

Since I do not wish to improvise, but to accept the Tradition of the Church, I would like to look at the characteristics of the orthodox mind of the Church as they are preserved in a text of a letter of the Apostle Paul. But we must point out that only the most characteristic things will be emphasised, while I do not exclude the existence of other characteristics.

The text that we shall study is from the Apostle Paul's epistle to the Ephesians, which, let it be said here, is regarded as the ecclesiological epistle 'par excellence', because it speaks about the Church. The Apostle writes:

"For this reason I bow my knees to the Father of our Lord Jesus Christ, from whom the whole family in heaven and earth is named, that he would grant you, according to the riches of his glory, to be strengthened with might through his Spirit in the inner man, that Christ may dwell in your hearts through faith; that you, being rooted and grounded in love, may be able to comprehend with all the saints what is the width and length and depth and height - to know the love of Christ which passes knowledge, that you may be filled with all the fullness of God.

"Now to him who is able to do exceeding abundantly above all that we ask or think, according to the power that works in us, to him be glory in the church by Christ Jesus throughout all ages, world without end. Amen". (Eph. 3, 14-21).

Analysing this apostolic passage, I would like us to look at seven characteristics which constitute the mind of the Orthodox Christian[1].

---

1. See analysis by Hieromonk Athanasios Gievtits: "The orthodox ecclesiastical ethos" in Witness of Orthodoxy (Gk.)

a) **Christological**

We are called Christians because through Baptism, the Divine Eucharist and the whole life which we live in the Church, which is the Body of Christ, we are really united with Christ. In the text which we have quoted above, the Apostle Paul says: "that Christ may dwell in your hearts through faith". "And to know the love of Christ which passes knowledge".

Influenced by Western notions, we consider that knowledge is connected more with the head and reason, and that faith is the simple acceptance of a hypothesesis. But in the Patristic Tradition faith is not a simple acceptance. To be sure, even this can be called an introductory faith, but faith is chiefly that which comes from vision of God, that is to say, man's unity with God. St. Isaac makes the distinction between the faith from hearing and the faith from seeing. The dwelling of Christ through faith is not independent of the illumination of the nous and the vision of God. Furthermore, this is also what constitutes real love and that true knowledge which is higher than the human created knowledge. The Fathers make a clear distinction between created and uncreated knowledge.

The fact that faith is connected with the man's union with Christ is seen in many patristic writings. St. Ignatios the Godbearer writes: "Perfect faith is Jesus Christ". St. Maximos teaches: "We say that Christ is faith personified". Our oneness with Christ is confirmed by the virtues, which are fruits of the Holy Spirit.

It is possible for men to have some virtues as a natural state. But this has not so much meaning as the virtues which are the fruit of the Holy Spirit, an expression of our union with Christ. For instance, atheists too can have self-control. But in the Church self-control and virginity have a different meaning and a different content. It is connected with man's depth, so we can speak of it as spiritual virginity. The same applies also to natural love. It is one thing for someone to love and be sensitive, and another thing for him to love when his nous is purified and he is a real member of the Body of Christ.

Therefore the orthodox mind of the Church is Christological, which means that the person who is characterised by it is united with Christ, belongs to His real Body, which is the Church, he experiences all the stages of the divine Economy. Thus the life in Christ is not an abstract ideology, but communion with Christ. Nor yet is it a humanistic life, but Christocentric par excellence. In the Church we do not believe in abstract values and ideas, but in virtues which are fruits of the Holy Spirit and a living of the uncreated energy of God, because love, peace, righteousness, etc., are natural or essential energies of God.

b) **Trinitarian**

But the so-called Christological life is not independent of the Trinitarian. We cannot consider Christ apart from the Holy Trinity, since Christ is the Second Person of the Holy Trinity and is united by nature with the Father and the Holy Spirit.

In the apostolic text which we are studying it is seen clearly. The Apostle Paul says: "I bow my knees to the Father of our Lord Jesus Christ... to be strengthened through his Spirit... that Christ may dwell... through faith...". Here we see the energy of the Persons of the Holy Trinity. Moreover, the salvation of man is a common activity of the Trinitarian God. The work of Christ and the work of the Holy

Spirit are not two different things. Christ became man by the good will of the Father and by the cooperation of the Holy Spirit. Christ sends the Holy Spirit who proceeds from the Father, and the Holy Spirit forms Christ in our hearts, and thus God the Father is glorified.

In the Church we experience the Trinitarian God. Holy Baptism takes place in the name of the Trinitarian God: "The servant of God is baptised in the name of the Father and the Son and the Holy Spirit". The Divine Eucharist is a glorification of the Trinitarian God: "Blessed is the Kingdom of the Father and the Son and the Holy Spirit". During the divine Eucharist we call upon the Father to send the Holy Spirit and change the bread and wine into the Body and Blood of Christ. The entire Christian life is a unity with the Holy Trinity, as St. Symeon the New Theologian says: "in which we have been baptised, by which we both live and know and understand, by which we are and shall be unto the ages of ages, as having had being and well being from it".

We live the energy of the Trinitarian God within us, because the Persons of the Holy Trinity have a common essence. The unity of the Persons of the Holy Trinity is due to the Person of the Father, but also to the common essence. Indeed, in speaking of the Trinitarian God, we say that there is no essence without hypostasis, nor hypostasis without essence. According to the Fathers, a person (hypostasis) may be defined as an essence "with individual characteristics", since the quality of the persons is immovable and invariable, and the communion of essence indivisible (St. Thalassios).

As we said in the beginning, the terms essence, hypostasis etc., are used by the Fathers in order to answer the ideas of the heretics, who were trying to explain philosophically the relationship of the Persons of the Holy Trinity. But the holy Fathers knew the relationships of the Persons of the Holy Trinity not from philosophy and conjecture, but from the personal experience which they had, from revelation.

There is one surprising witness of St. Symeon the New Theologian on this subject. Speaking of the experience of the Holy Trinity which he had, he says that he saw three lights. And we know both from the witness of this saint and from other witnesses that during the experience of the Holy Trinity the deified person sees not the essence, but the energy, and indeed one light endowed with flesh, another light which is not endowed with flesh, and a third, which is the source of the two preceding ones. The Father is the light which is the souce of the other Lights, the Son is a Light endowed with flesh, and the Holy Spirit is not a body, but is a Light which has its cause in the first Light. The saints express this experience by the terms "essence" - "hypostasis" in order to deny the heretical ideas which were circulating in their time and to place the terms where they separate error and truth. Moreover, it must be said that this faith is essentially a matter of experience.

The orthodox-ecclesiastical mind is not distinguished by an abstract and sentimental faith in Christ or in an abstract and general God, but in the Father, Son and Holy Spirit. And our prayer should refer to this particular God.

c) Ecclesiological

But Christ cannot be separated from the Church, which is His true Body. Some people maintain that we should love Christ, but not the Church which distorted Christ's teaching. But this is an erroneous position.

In the text which we are studying it says characteristically: "to him be glory in the church by Christ Jesus throughout all ages". Here it seems that the glory of God is manifested in the Church. Thus the orthodox-ecclesiastical mind is ecclesiological.

Indeed it must be noted that the Church exists also in the Old Testament. Furthermore, St. John Chrysostom observes that Christ by His incarnation "took flesh of the church". On this subject there is much patristic mention, as we saw in another chapter. The fact is that, according to the teaching of the holy Fathers, we have the Church through the creation of the angels and of man. Then there is the fall of Adam and Eve, and yet the Church in the Old Testament is saved by the Prophets and the deified. By the incarnation of Christ, however, the Church has a Body. It is the Body of Christ.

Here I would like to cite only two patristic texts. One is from Clement of Rome. He says: "spiritual being was created before the sun and the moon; but the spiritual was made manifest in the flesh of Christ". Athanasios the Great too writes characteristically: "First created and then born of God". Thus the Church now is the Body of Christ. And of course when we say Church we do not mean something abstract, but the members of the Church, because the Apostle Paul says: "Now you are the body of Christ, and members individually" (1 Cor. 12,27).

Christ, then is inseparable from the Church, whose head He is, and the Church is inseparable from Christ, whose Body it is. That is why it is in the Church that the glory of God is also preserved and made manifest and it is in the Church that we attain participation in this glory. In the Church we are baptised, because holy Baptism is the introductory sacrament, in the Church we receive communion of the Body and Blood of Christ and in the Church we participate in the incarnation, Cross and Resurrection of Christ.

This means that we remain in the Church to attain our salvation. We receive the whole teaching of the Fathers and seek to adapt our life in this direction. We do not break away from the Church, that is to say from the canonical Hierarchy and our saints, who are the bearers of the Tradition. We do not strive to save the Church, because the Church, which is the Body of Christ, does not need saviours, but we struggle to be saved as we remain in the Church.

d) Esoteric

But when we speak of the life which we possess in the Church, we must observe that we live this life in our heart. The mind of the Orthodox Christian is not turned outward, it does not remain on the surface, but it is an inner life, of the heart. It refers to the inner man. It says in the text which we are studying: "to be strengthened through his Spirit in the inner man, that Christ may dwell in your hearts through faith". Here it is emphasised that we experience Christ in our hearts, Christ dwells there. And this must be placed in the teaching which we mentioned in the beginning about the mind of the spirit.

Today much is being said about the person. We give different definitions. There are two definitions of person. One is more philosophical, it accepts that every man is a person and determines some characteristic features of the person. The other is ecclesiological and attempts to see the ecclesiastical dimension of the person. Indeed it is said that man as an ecclesiastical being transcends his so-called biological hypostasis and this makes him a person par excellence. There are elements of truth in these interpretations. But I would like to observe that the asceticism of the person is not being examined. Moreover, in the patristic tradition the man par excellence, the person par excellence, is he who has noetic energy, who is turned towards God, in other words, he who has an illuminated nous and unceasing prayer.

The person is not independent of the regeneration of man, which takes place in the inner region and then stretches outward as well. A person in reality is "the hidden person of the heart with the incorruptible ornament of a gentle and quiet spirit, which is very precious in the sight of God" (1 Peter 3, 4).

The text which we are studying speaks about the inner man and about Christ who dwells in our hearts. The orthodox-ecclesiastical mind is inward, is of the heart.

The heart is that place which is revealed by asceticism in grace and in which God Himself is revealed. The Apostle Paul says: "the love of God has been poured out in our hearts by the Holy Spirit who was given to us" (Rom. 5, 5). It is in the heart that the union of man with God takes place and it is there that man attains knowledge of God. St. Gregory the Theologian speaks of "God united to gods and known in the heart". The entrance to the Kingdom of God is not independent of the heart filled with grace by the Holy Spirit. St. Mark the Ascetic writes: "it is necessary first to have the grace of the Holy Spirit acting in the heart and thus correspondingly to enter into the Kingdom of heaven". In the neptic* tradition of the Church the heart is characterised as the holy of holies, as a temple where the true priest of divine grace functions as the receptacle of the blessings, as the natural monastery.

Therefore the orthodox-ecclesiastical mind is not connected with emotional states, but with the real experiences and the regenerated life which is experienced in the heart. This is attained through deep and complete repentance, through prayer of the nous in the heart.

e) Deification

The Christian's aim, towards which his whole life is directed and with which all his activities are imbued, is deification. This is accentuated in the apostolic text which we are studying. The Apostle Paul writes: "that you may be filled with all the fullness of God". "That he would grant you according to the riches of his glory". But also all the other places which speak of Christ's coming and dwelling in the heart are synonymous with deification.

The word 'theosis', or deification, is patristic, and it is not mentioned in Holy Scripture. But there are other synonymous words in Holy Scripture which express the content of deification. One of these is 'doxasmos', glorification. For a member of the Church to be glorified does not mean to be honoured, but to partake of the uncreated glory of God, which is to be deified. This is also said in the text which we are studying: "That he would grant you, according to the riches of his glory", and also "that you may be filled with all the fullness of God".

Fullness is the attainment of, or better, participation in the age of the fullness of Christ. And at another point the Apostle Paul says: "till we all come... to a perfect man, to the measure of the stature of the fullness of Christ" (Eph. 4, 13). That we should attain the stature of Christ does not mean that we should reach the bodily age of Christ, but that we should experience His whole life within our own being. That is to say that we should live the circumcision,

Cross, Passion, Burial, Resurrection and Assumption of Christ. St. Gregory the Theologian is characteristic when he emphasises epigrammatically: "Travel without fault as a disciple of Christ through every stage and faculty of His life; be purified, be circumcised... be crucified with Him, and share His death and burial gladly, that you may rise with Him, and be glorified with Him and reign with Him". By endeavouring to mortify our earthly limbs, that is to say, the passions, in combination with the sacramental and ascetic life of the Church we live the Cross and the Passion of Christ and have the assurance that we shall also live His Resurrection and Assumption.

Therefore the orthodox-ecclesiastical mind is not exhausted in a few social, external and superficial deeds, but it refers to deification. All the pastoral guidance, as well as the catechetical endeavour of the Church, is aimed at the deification of man. From this point of view the ecclesiastical life is distinct from any other religious life.

f) Personal and social

Previously we spoke about the person who is developed and lives in the heart. Now we must say that the orthodox-ecclesiastical mind also extends to the outside. When a man really becomes a person, then he develops real communion with God and man. Thus he becomes social, he loves all men.

We use the word "social" in another sense. The Christian, living in the Church in communion with the Trinitarian God and travelling towards deification, is living also with the saints. In the text which we are studying it says: "that you may be able to comprehend with all the saints what is the width and length and depth and height - to know the love of Christ which passes knowledge". In the Church we live "with all the saints". We are saved by the saints and have communion with them.

Saints, according to St. Symeon the New Theologian, are "those who have acquired the whole Christ within them wholly by work and experience and perception and knowledge and vision of God". From this witness it seems clear that saintliness does not have an abstract and ethical meaning. Saintliness is participation in the uncreated deifying energy of God, and the person deified is a saint. Saints are those who have experience and knowledge and perception and vision of God. They are not simply the good people.

Living in the Church we have communion with the saints, that is to say, either we have the same life with them and perceive our brotherhood in Christ or, if we do not have the same experience as they, nevertheless we follow their teaching. We attune our teaching to the teaching of the saints and the Councils in which the saints took part. Therefore we do not have our own conjectures.

In the "Council of Orthodoxy" we confess among other things: "that the Prophets saw, the Apostles taught, the Church received, the teachers taught, the world agreed... so we think, so we say, so we proclaim Christ to be our true God. This faith of the Apostles, this faith of the Fathers, this faith of the Orthodox, this faith supported the world".

The Prophets, Apostles and holy men throughout the ages are saints. These words of St. Gregory Palamas are characteristic: "This is saving perfection in both knowledge and doctrines, the same was thought by the prophets, apostles, fathers, by simply everyone through whom the Holy Spirit bears witness. And the great confessor of Orthodoxy, St. Athanasios says that all the saints "agree and do not differ with one another", even if they lived in different times. Terminology changes, but not the content of the teaching and the Revelation which all the Prophets, Apostles and saints received. According to Athanasios the Great it is unsuitable for us to think that there is a conflict between the Fathers. Also it is not God-fearing for us to say that some of the Fathers spoke well and others not.

So let us attune our lives to the life and teaching of the Prophets, Apostles and saints. Then we will be characterised by an ecclesiastical mind.

g) **Prayerful**

Finally, the orthodox-ecclesiastical mind is a mind which is imbued with prayer. It is, we would say, prayerful. The whole apostolic text which we are studying is a text of prayer. It begins with the sentence: For this cause I bow my knees to the Father of our Lord Jesus Christ" and it ends: "to him be glory in the church by Christ Jesus throughout all ages".

The Orthodox Christian prays to God. And he is especially distinguished for unceasing inner prayer of the heart. This prayer is a doxology, a thanksgiving, an entreaty, a confession. All the things that we do should be made holy by prayer. Then we are showing that they, and ourselves too, are genuine.

There is a close relationship between prayer and divine Eucharist. The more a person prays, the more his thirst for divine Communion increases, and the more he communes of the undefiled Mysteries, the more his thirst and zeal for prayer increases. Theology is closely connected with prayer and especially noetic prayer.

Summing up, we may say that the genuine orthodox-ecclesiastical mind is that which is Christological, Trinitarian, ecclesiological, of the heart, divine, social, in prayer.

To be sure, all these are not external to one another, but there is a wonderful unity. Furthermore, the whole of orthodox theology resembles a circle. At whatever point you touch it, it connects with the whole circle. The Christological is at the same time Trinitarian and ecclesiological. The ecclesiological is prayerful, divine, and within the heart and social. It is not possible for one of them to exist without the others.

We live in an epoch in which there is conflict on this subject. Some of them accuse the others of not having the mind of the Church. I think that we should reflect on this apostolic text with the patristic analysis which we have made, so as to see whether we are characterised by the genuine orthodox mind of the Church. And this will not be an occasion for boasting, but essential for salvation. For outside this atmosphere there is uncertainty about salvation.

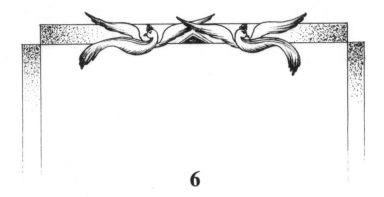

6

The Catholic way of life

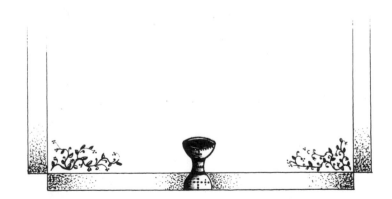

The Catholic way of life

One of the characteristics of the Church, as is confessed in the Creed, is catholicity. We confess that the Church is "catholic".

The catholicity of the Church has three particular meanings. One is that it extends over the whole world. St. Kyril of Jerusalem confesses: "It is called catholic because it exists diffused throughout world". The second is that the Church has the fullness of truth and helps the person who is its member to share in the whole fullness of the truth, to experience the whole truth. The Church has lived the truth since the day of Pentecost. Since Pentecost the Church has not increased in truth, but the faithful participate and progress personally in Pentecost and in the experience of the Revelation. Pentecost is the highest degree of divine Revelation. Through the ages we have the expression of the truth in various terms in order to confront the heretics. Thus a catholic man is one who recognises the truth (Orthodox) and lives the truth (righteous). And the third meaning is that the Church is called Catholic because it has a life which is common to all its members. In the Church there are no privileged and unprivileged members. The ministries and gifts differ, but all are able to apply Christ's commandments and all have the ability to attain the experience of Pentecost. The Apostle Paul declares: "as many of you as were baptised in Christ have put on Christ. There is neither Jew nor Greek, there is neither slave nor free, there is neither male nor female, for you are all one in Christ Jesus" (Gal. 3, 27-28).

In what follows we shall study chiefly this third case. We shall look into the fact that the life which exists in the Church can be experienced by all its members, that there is one catholic way of life, there are no splittings in the Church, nor various categories of people who have different tasks and obligations. Moreover, each person is created by God in His image and likeness. And if we think that the likeness in the theology of the holy Fathers is essentially identical with deification, then we can infer that every person, and especially every member of the Church, has the possibility of attaining deification.

1. The fall and restoration of man

I think that it is well for us to begin the subject by studying the fall of man and his resurrection which took place in Christ. This is very important, because in this way we shall be able to look more broadly at our subject, the catholic way of life. It is important also because the subject of the fall and resurrection is the basis of soteriology. If we do not examine it scientifically, we shall never be able to understand and live the life which the Church has. I ought to mention that the question of what is the fall of man has been analysed in other books of mine, and I do not want to repeat it. I shall merely emphasise a few points. The reader can find an extensive analysis in my book "Orthodox Psychotherapy", and in "Time to act", in the chapter "Traditional Catechism".

We usually think of the fall in juridical terms, in meaning which have been taken from the law courts. We consider that Adam's sin was simply a transgression of a law, an external one, and that this transgression created great guilt in man, with the result that this guilt has been inherited in Adam's descendants.

But this view of sin is not orthodox. In Orthodoxy we regard sin as an illness of man. Man fell ill and this illness had an effect on the whole human race. St. Kyril of Alexandria uses the image of the plant. When the root of the plant has become ill, then the branches also fall ill. We can interpret Adam's sin in this way as well.

St. Maximos, speaking of the fall of man and his restoration, puts them on a theological basis. He says that at the creation of the world and of man there were five divisions. The division between uncreated and created, noetic and tangible, Heaven and earth, Paradise and world, male and female. Adam, by the grace of God, but also by his personal struggle, an expression of his freedom, would have to overcome these divisions and reach communion and unity with the uncreated. To be sure, this last division, that between created and uncreated, could not be abolished, but the created would attain unity with the uncreated. Moreover, in the Church we say that there is no division between physical and metaphysical things, as philosophy claimed, but between created and uncreated. And further, we accept that the uncreated enters into the created, and thus man himself, as St. Maximos the Confessor says, also becomes uncreated by grace. Adam failed to transcend these divisions. And not only did he fail to transcend the division which we mentioned, but he also lost the purity which existed between the two sexes, with the result that decay and mortality entered into nature, that he wore the coats of skin of decay and mortality. Therefore now man's way of conception, gestation, birth, etc., is a result of the fall, it is what the Fathers called coats of skin, which he wore after the fall.

The transcending of the five divisions took place in Christ. By His incarnation, by His birth from a Virgin, by the union of divine and human nature, he united the uncreated with the created, the heavenly with the earth, the noetic with the sensible, Paradise with the world, and he even transcended the division between male and female. Thus man's restoration was successful and every person was given the possibility that in Christ he too could transcend all the divisions and achieve his salvation.

If we want to look more concretely at the matter of the fall we will say that, as St. John of Damaskos teaches, the fall in reality is darkness of the image, loss of the divine life and putting on the coats of skin. The darkness of the image is nothing else but the darkening of the nous. The nous was darkened and could not have communion and unity with God. Of course it must be said that according to the anthropology of the Fathers, man's soul is rational and noetic. This means that man has two centres of functioning. One is the reasoning mind, which is connected with his nervous system, and the other his nous, which is connected with his heart. Adam's fall, then, is the darkening of his nous, the loss of its noetic function, confusion of the nous with the functions of reason and its enslavement to the passions and to the environment. Instead of moving according to nature and above nature, instead of moving towards God and being mindful of God, man's nous is turned towards the created things and the passions. That is why in the Church we speak of repentance, which is not simply a change in the head, as some theologians say, but a change of the nous. The nous must break away from the created and the passions and turn towards God.

A result of the darkening of his noetic energy is that man's relationship with God and his fellow man is upset. Because of his darkened nous, man does not find meaning in life, he turns his attention to the external things, with the result that he comes to blows with men, he has no inner peace. This is analysed in a wonderful way by St. Gregory Palamas. Fallen man uses God to safeguard his individual security and regards his neighbour as an object for predatory exploitation. He cannot have selfless love, because all his expressions and all his love contain the element of self-seeking, which is to say that man is characterised by self-seeking love. So the darkening of the nous has drastic social consequences. Sociology cannot be regarded as independent of theology.

In this sense we can speak of inheritance of sin and of the ancestral sin, which man inherits at birth. In this sense too we can speak of the catholicity of the fall of man.

What Adam failed to do, Christ, who is called the new Adam, succeeded in doing. By His incarnation Christ deified human nature and became the strongest medicine for men, in the sense that He gave every man the possibility of achieving his deification. In this light we can interpret the phrase from the troparion that Christ raised up "Adam with the whole human race".

At this point I would like to look at two passages in St. John of Damaskos which will help us to understand in some way the mystery of the incarnation of the Second Person of the Holy Trinity. It must of course be emphasised that this too is a subject not of rational understanding but of spiritual experience, yet we can say something about the doctrine of the incarnation of the Son and Word of God.

St. John of Damaskos, repeating a passage from St. Gregory the Theologian whom he calls his spiritual father, says that Christ took on the whole human nature, because what is not assumed is not cured. St. John of Damaskos goes on to say that the ruling centre of the soul and the flesh is the nous, which is the purest part of the soul, but also that the ruling centre of the nous is God Himself. When God acts, then the nous manifests its own authority, and then "it is under the control of the stronger and follows it, doing those things which the divine will desires". The Son and Word of God has united with the flesh "by means of the nous", which is midway between the purity of God and the grossness of the flesh. So the nous became the place of its personal union with divinity. The saint writes characteristically: "The nous becomes the seat of the Divinity which has been hypostatically united to it". This has great importance, because it shows that man's salvation begins and works in the nous and then extends to the whole body. Thus we understand the great importance of the neptic tradition of our Church.

The other point from the teaching of St. John of Damaskos which is useful to us here is that by His incarnation the Word of God did not assume the human nature "that is understood in pure theory", that is to say, he did not assume a simple nature, that which is seen externally, because then it would not have been incarnation, but an illusion and fiction of incarnation. Also He did not assume this nature "regarded as a species", but that which is seen in the individual, which at the same time belongs also to the species, because Christ assumed the whole mixture of what was our own from the beginning. This is important because, as St. John of Damaskos again says, human nature rose from the dead and sat at the right hand of the

Father "not implying that all human persons arose and sat at the right hand of the Father, but that our entire nature did so in the Person of Christ". That is to say that human nature has been deified in the person of the Logos. So human nature has been deified in the hypostasis of the Logos, but our own human hypostases must be deified as well.

Therefore the catholicity of Adam's fall has the meaning of the illness of human nature and the catholicity of the resurrection through the New Adam, Christ, it again has the meaning of the cure. Christ cured human nature, He Himself became the strongest medicine towards the cure, and he gives every man the possibility of being cured. Thus we can maintain that Christ is both the physician and the medicine, man's cure and his health.

2. Making salvation one's own

From what we have said it is seen that all men have the possibility of being deified. There are no privileged categories that can travel towards deification. The cure and deification of man is achieved, on the one hand, by the sacramental life, and on the other hand, by the ascetic life which we live in the Church.

I would like to emphasise this fact particularly. All the holy Fathers teach that man's salvation is a combination of sacraments and asceticism. We cannot understand the sacraments without asceticism in Christ, and we cannot live a real ascetic life without the sacraments of the Church. Moreover, the whole life in the Church is an experience of a great mystery. Asceticism is in reality experience of the commandments of Christ which is attained by partaking in the purifying, illuminating and deifying energy of God. Insofar as anyone experiences the purifying, illuminating and deifying energy of God, he is experiencing rightly the sacramental life.

I say this because in our time a great deal is being said about the sacramental life, the eucharistiological life is being much emphasised. This is very good. But, unfortunately, the ascetic tradition of the Church is being overlooked. St. Gregory Palamas, as well as all the other Fathers, was a catholic theologian, and therefore he made a parallel struggle against the Massalians who overemphasised the hesychastic life at the expense of the sacraments, and against Barlaam, who overemphasised the sacramental life at the expense of the hesychastic life. This is essential to be emphasised.

The beginning of our experience of salvation is achieved by holy Baptism, which is also called an introductory sacrament, because it introduces us to the life of the Church, which is life in Christ at the same time. But in the early Church Baptism was preceded by purification. The exorcisms also have this meaning.

Apart from others who refer to other books on this subject, here I must emphasise that the Fathers of the Local Synod in Antioch specify that the country bishops should not ordain Priests and Deacons without the permission of the Bishop of the city, but only to appoint "Readers, Subdeacons and Exorcists". And St. Nikodemos the Hagiorite*, interpreting what the exorcists are, says that they are the catechists. He writes characteristically: "The name of exorcists is given to the catechists of those faithless or heretics who are coming into the faith, because in catechising them, they exorcise the evil spirits dwelling in them, in the name of the Lord, that they should leave them, and this is evident, sometimes from those sons of the Evil spirit who called the name of the Lord into the demonised, saying to the demons, we exorcise you in the name of Jesus, whom Paul proclaimed (Acts 19,12); sometimes also from the exorcisms where the Priest reads to those who are about to be baptised".

So it seems that the Catechumens go through the stage of purification and the Catechists were the exorcists who had the special blessing of the Church to do this work. Through catechesis the catechumens passed the stage of purification, when by holy Baptisms and by Chrismation they experienced the illuminating energy of God, discovered their nous, their noetic energy moved naturally and supranaturally, and for this reason Baptism is called illumination.

If we study the New Testament carefully, especially the Epistles of the Apostle Paul, we shall we convinced that really it is speaking about purification, illumination and deification. Some passages refer to the stage of purification, some to the stage of illumination and others to the stage of deification. I do not choose to make an analysis of this point here. I only wish to underline that the things said about purification, illumination and deification are not an influence from ancient Greek philosophy, but an experience of the Christians, which can be discovered also in the texts of Holy Scripture.

At all events it is a fact that all people have the possibility of attaining deification, provided that all are catechised members of the Church and then baptised and anointed and have the possibility of Holy Communion. Hence, in the Church there is one common way of life, relatively speaking, of course.

With Baptism and Chrismation a new life begins. But this life must be continued and increased. This new life is expressed and energised by three basic factors: by applying the commandments of Christ, by divine Communion and by prayer.

The commandments of Christ are mentioned at all the points on man's journey towards deification. We have been accustomed to regarding the commandments as legalistic orders, to which we must adapt our life. Without excluding even one such means of adapting, we emphasise that God's commandments are medicines to help us to be cured in our souls. St. Dionysios the Areopagite says that our union with God is achieved "only by love and holy work". And of course Christ's commandments refer to many topics, such as to the divine Liturgy. The celebration of the Divine Liturgy is an application of Christ's commandment: "this do in remembrance of me...".

Still, the divine Communion leads a person to deification. Of course we must add that divine Communion deifies man when he is in this state. Otherwise it illuminates him, purifies him, while if he has not repented and has not entered the stage of purification, it burns him up, condemns him. This is why Nikolas Kavasilas, interpreting the Apostle Paul's "if someone does not want to work, let him not eat", says that this is true not only for material bread, but also for the spiritual bread. He who does not wish to work and to practise asceticism spiritually should not approach the Holy Table and receive Holy Communion.

But also prayer, especially that which is called noetic prayer, is that which expresses the new life which man attains through Baptism and helps him to increase it, because according to the teaching of the holy Fathers, there is no limit and boundary to perfection and virtue. The passage of the Apostle Paul "be filled with the Spirit, speaking to one another in psalms and hymns and spiritual songs, singing and making melody in your heart to the Lord" (Eph.

5, 18-19) refers to noetic prayer, which goes on in the heart with hymns and psalms and spiritual songs, by the energy of the Holy Spirit. The connection of prayer with the Holy Spirit and with the heart indicates the existence of noetic prayer which goes on unceasingly, and therefore we have the commandment to pray without ceasing.

3. The catholic way of life

All that has been said indicates that the Christian who is baptised in the Name of the Trinitarian God should live the new life as a result, and this is achieved through applying the commandments of Christ, through holy Communion and through prayer. But these things refer to all people. All people should be directed towards this aim. There are no people who by nature cannot do the will of God, by nature cannot pray. If there were, God would not be so hard as to demand the same things from all.

St. John Chrysostom, speaking of the raising of children, and having in mind parents who did not advise their children to do the whole will of God, on the excuse that this applies to monks, said characteristically: From the very first "Bring him up in the chastening and admonition of the Lord". And immediately he added: "Never say, this is the business of monks. Am I making a monk of him? No. There is no need for him to become a monk. Why be so afraid of a thing so replete with so much advantage? Make him a Christian". The keeping of Christ's commandments does not refer only to monks, but to the Christian in general. Our Christian quality, if we can express it that way, entails the keeping of Christ's commandments.

Thus the Christian's way of life is catholic. All the Christians must have a common ethos. The aim of Christ's commandments and the holy Canons of the Church is for Christians to attain this common ethos, this uniform life.

To be sure, I must also emphasise for us to keep in view about the things said further on, that while all of us can keep the commandments of God and have the aim of deification, there are different degrees, but also different ways. The path is the same, but the way varies according to the way in which each person lives. We can understand this from the Parable of the talents. Some received five talents, some two, some one. But all can prove to be proportionally good administrators and good stewards of divine grace, and all can hear the "Well done, thou good and faithful servant". The quantity of talents differs, but the same word of blessing will be heard. So there is a variety of gifts, proportional to people's way of life and spiritual maturity. The fact is that there is a common life and all have to tread the same path of salvation.

But unfortunately, since we are fragmentary and, what is worse, since we want to remain fragmentary and on low levels of spiritual life because they suit us, we create fragments and divisions in the spiritual life.

In what follows I would like us to look at a few such divisions which we create in our thought and life.

a) Theologians and non-theologians

We divide people into theologians and non-theologians. We consider that theologians are those who possess some intellectual knowledge, and we think that theology is a speciality of some people who are studying scientifically the history of the Church. Without excluding the possibility that this too may be one distinction between students and teachers, we must say that theology is chiefly life, ex-

perience, and that theologians, according to the teaching
of the Church, are essentially those who see God.

St. Gregory the Theologian says that theologians are
"those who have been examined and are passed masters in
the vision of God", which is to say those who have been
tested and purified and, as a result, reached deification. Likewise, according to St. Neilos, a theologian is one who prays.
Therefore theologians are those who experience the purifying, especially the illuminating and deifying energy of God.

Thus one person can have completed theological school,
taught theology, and yet not know experientially what theology is. And another person can be mentally illiterate, but
have developed his noetic energy to the extreme, and be a
real theologian. On the Holy Mountain one can meet such
people, who are aale to interpret and analyse the teaching
of the holy Fathers of the Church.

b) Neptic and social theology

We divide theology into neptic and social, and we regard some Fathers as belonging to the first and others as
belonging to the second category. But in the teaching of
the holy Fathers this division is not seen. To be sure, out-
waradly, from the way in which each one has worked, a
division can be seen between the neptics and socials, because some Fathers had a particular flock and did their
work there, and others were in the desert, praying constantly. Even from this aspect, however, there cannot be a
perfect division, because even the Fathers who worked
pastorally lived neptically, and the hermits worked in a
missionary way, in the sense that they were magnets for
many men who approached them to learn "words" of salvation. Thus the hermits indirectly did pastoral work.

Beyond this, the teaching of the saints is not divided into social and neptic. When the Fathers speak of social topics, they look at them within the true theology of the Church, which is ascetic. And when they speak of neptic topics, they do it in order for people to be able to be purified and then to attain real communion with God and men. Besides, we know very well that in the Church the theologians do shepherding and the pastors do their work theologically.

We are accustomed to seeing the Three Hierarchs, Basil the Great, Gregory the Theologian and Chrysostom as social Fathers. But this does not correspond with reality, because the Three Hierarchs in their writings also explain the whole neptic teaching of the Church.

The fact that there is a close link between nepsis and communion, between neptic and social Fathers, and that the holy Fathers shepherd their flocks theologically is seen from the homilies written by St. Gregory Palamas to his flock in Thessaloniki. Anyone who reads these homilies will discover that shepherding is theology and theology is truly a fruit of the knowledge of God, but also a path for man to reach deification.

c) Action (praxis) and theoria (vision of God)

A result of the foregoing is that we usually make a distinction between action and theoria, as well as between practical and theoretical people. This distinction is made because the western distinction of action and contemplation has influenced us.

In the West according to Mesaiona, they speak of theory and practice, the latter meaning mission, action, while the former is intellectual occupation with God and the truths of the Church. In the Orthodox Tradition, however, action is chiefly purification of the heart, and theoria is noetic prayer and the vision of the uncreated Light, the deification of man.

Likewise, in the Orthodox Church we say that action and theoria of God are not opposites, but one follows the other. Ilias the Presbyter says that the courageous man is like a woman who keeps two lamps burning, "mastering both action and theoria". St. Maximos the Confessor says that there is no safe action without theoria, nor true theoria without action. "For action needs to be learned and theoria put into practice". And he points out that in some the theoria is preceded by action and in others action is preceded by theoria, but finally both have to end in one thing".

d) Mystical and ascetic life

Yet many of us separate the mystical from the ascetic life. We think that the Sacraments are chiefly for those who live in the world, while asceticism is for the monks. But there is no such distinction in the Patristic teaching, for as we have previously analysed, the Sacraments are not independent of the experience of God's purifying, illuminating and deifying energy. As Father John Romanides points out, medical science cannot be separated from diagnosis and therapy. And the diagnosis and the therapy cannot in any way degenerate into several external ceremonial acts. In the same way the divine Liturgy and prayer cannot be separated from purification of the heart and illumination of the nous.

e) Apophatic (negative) and cataphatic (positive) theology

We make a further watertight distinction between apophatic and cataphatic theology. We insist that apophatic theology is more perfect, while cataphatic is imperfect. Still the worst is when we see apophatic theology only in the existence of a few terms and expressions.

True, in the patristic teaching we encounter such a division. The expression of St. John of Damaskos is characteristic: "The Divinity, then, is limitless and incomprehensible, and His limitlessness and incomprehensibility is all that can be understood about Him. All that we state affirmatively about God does not show His nature, but only what relates to His nature". But then again St. John of Damaskos says: "Moreover, there are things that are stated affirmatively of God, but which have the force of extreme negation".

There is an interpenetration between apophatic and cataphatic theology. Theology is one, and it is experience, revelation. The saints attained deification and saw God. They saw that God is Light, they saw God's energy. Thus God is participated in with regard to His energy, but He is altogether unshared by man with regard to His essence. But when the saints wish to express this experience, they use negative figures. They say, for instance, that God is Light, but at the same time add, "because of His surpassing brightness" also in relation to the created light of knowledge. it is "darkness". Moreover, even the so-called affirmative expressions, such as that God is love, in reality are impossible for human reason to understand, in the terms of human thought and employing representations.

We can say that the knowledge of God is experience.

The way to knowledge of God is apophatic, which means that we concentrate our nous in our heart, following, according to St. Dionysios the Areopagite, the uniform concentration of the nous. The experience of God, of God's energy, is positive. But the expression of this experience is formulated also by negative expressions ("invisible", "incomprehensible", "indescribable" etc.), because of man's inability to express this experience.

f) Monks and married people

We divide people further into monks and married people, and life into monastic and married, with the result that we praise the monastic life, which we regard as better and more suited to keeping God's commandments, while we disparage married life as not suitable for the practice of God's will.

Indeed we know very well that the Church praises both ways of life, both the monastic life and the married life. But this does not mean that one is praised at the expense of the other. And at this point we must say that the interpretation of the Parable of the talents applies, which we mentioned before.

It can be maintained that in the Church the people are not divided simply into unmarried and married, but into people who live in Christ and people who do not live in Christ. Thus on the one hand we have people who have the Holy Spirit and on the other hand people who do not have the Holy Spirit. Moreover, in the first Church, as it seems in the Epistles of the Apostle Paul, all the Christians, unmarried and married, lived like monks, because even marriage has its asceticism. Therefore, if some monk criticises marriage in Christ, he shows that he has a problem with the monastic life, and if a married person criticises and looks askance at the monastic life, it means that he has a problem with the way in which he is living his life. A good monk never criticises what God praises and a good married person never criticises anything that God praises, such as the monastic life. It is characteristic that the best homily about Virginity is said to have been composed by St. Gregory of Nyssa, who was married: and a man who was unmarried, St. Amphilochios of Ikonio, wrote excellent things about the married life. Moreover let us not forget that St. Paphnoutios defended marriage for the Clergy in the First Ecumenical Council.

In his homily St. Amphilochios of Ikonio shows that the Christian is a catholic man, in other words, whole. He praises virginity and marriage. In speaking about virginity he says of marriage: "the worthy marriage towers above every earthly gift, such as a tree in fruit... as a root of virginity, as a cultivator of the rational and living branches". Then he says: "remove the worthy marriage and you do not find the flower of virginity". Moreover, the comparison is between two worthy things, because St. Amphilochios says: "Saying these things, we are not introducing a fight between virginity and marriage; we admire both as mutually indebted". To conclude, he says characteristically: "For without devout knowledge of divine things neither is virginity modest nor marriage worthy".

And the holy Chrysostom teaches many things about this subject. He says: "For our married people have everything in common with the monks except marriage". All people should adapt themselves to Christ's commandments. Therefore the holy Father says characteristically: "If we are temperate neither marriage nor nourishment nor anything else will prevent us from being able to be well-pleasing to God". If marriage and raising children was going to hinder us on the path of virtue, the creator of all things would not have brought marriage into our life".

What Basil the Great says is also characteristic: "We people, monks and married, are all required to obey the Gospel.

Therefore we cannot justify our indolence by the particular way of life which we have chosen, nor can we criticise and dismiss another way of life which is not like our own. To be sure, there are degrees and spiritual ages.

g) Monasteries and Parishes

This is also connected with the distinction which we create between the Monasteries and the Parishes. Usually we create conflicts and splits between these two centres of life.

But in Orthodoxy we say that there is a relationship between the Parishes and the Monasteries. St. John Chrysostom urges his listeners to visit the Monasteries to see the earthly angels, as he calls the monks, so that then they can live a sound community and family life.

The Monastery and the Parish are the two centres of Christian life. The Monasteries are nourished by the Parishes, and then they help the Parishes in their way. St. Kosmas the Aitolian grew spiritually mature on the Holy Mountain and then became a great missionary. Bishop Nektarios of Pentapolis created a Monastery, and through this Monastery he helped the people. To honour St. Nektarios and criticise monasticism, in which he lived, does not constitute an orthodox ethos, it is a splitting of the catholicity of the Church and a spiritual schizophrenia.

h) Monks and Missionaries

A result of the preceding is that, unfortunately, we make a split between the charismatics, between monks and missionaries. Some think that the monks by their praying do not achieve any work in society, and others undervalue the missionary effort which other Christians make.

However, things are not so simple. Many are the gifts which the Holy Spirit gives for the building up of the Body of Christ. We must value and accept the gifts which are given by the Holy Spirit. To undervalue one gift is blasphemy, according to St. Symeon the New Theologian.

At another point in his teaching St. Symeon the New Theologian says that many people regarded the desert life as happy, some the coenobitic life, and for others happiness was to govern the people, to legislate, teach and establish Churches: "But I would not wish to give preference to any of these states or exalt one type of life and discredit another. In all walks of life, whatever our work and activities, blessed is the life lived for God and according to God".

It is not a matter of the work we do in the Church, but of whether we do it by the inspiration of the Holy Spirit, whether we perform it in the fear of God and whether we are aiming at the glory of God. Then, whatever this work is, it is blessed and will have eternal results. Otherwise our work will be burned (1 Cor. 3, 12-15).

i) Clergy and laymen

Another distinction which we make is between Clergy and laymen. That there is such a distinction and it belongs to the whole Tradition of the Church, no one can deny. But on this point too we cannot overvalue one category at the expense of the other. Nothing of the sort constitutes the orthodox mind. Nor can we consider that only the Clergy are obligated to keep all the Laws and Traditions of the Church, while the laymen have some mitigations. It is a fact that the Clergy have more duties and obligations in relation to salvation and other things, but all have the duty to keep God's Law.

We can say that the Church's system of government is synodal. This should not be interpreted in the sense of democracy. Some people say that the Church's system of government is democratic. This is not so, because there is a distinction of gifts and ministries. The Church's system of government is synodical, in the sense of hierarchy; that is to say, it is hierarchical. This is seen in the Apostle Paul's letter to the Corinthians. The Apostle says: "And God has appointed these in the church: first apostles, second prophets, third teachers, after that miracles, then gifts of healings, helps, administrations, varieties of tongues" (1 Cor. 12, 28). Thus there is a hierarchy in the Church. Each person knows his gift, fulfills the service which God assigned, and all work together for the edifice of the Body of Christ. The image of the Body of Christ is very characteristic!

The Clergy are ordained to serve and minister to the people. It is a gift from God for someone to shepherd, it is a gift to be shepherded towards one's salvation. Moreover, the base of the sacramental priesthood is what is called spiritual priesthood, which laymen too can have. Everyone can have spiritual priesthood, because it is connected with the whole spiritual life, which is experienced through both the Sacraments and asceticism. According to the Fathers, the person has spiritual priesthood who has developed his noetic energy, and of course, who prays for the whole world. And we know that this spiritual priesthood will make a man worthy of enjoying the Kingdom of God.

Thus there should be no quarrel between Clergy and laymen. The Clergy receive the priesthood as a ministry and a sacrifice on the cross and the laymen accept the Clergy as fathers in order to be reborn into a new life.

I shall not go on to mention further distinctions which, unfortunately, we make in our spiritual and ecclesiastical life. The malevolent man, who is split, splits up the united life of the Church. As far as a man is impure, so far he is also in pieces, as far as he is purified of passion so far he is catholic. He is made catholic when he knows and experiences the whole truth. The whole way of life, which we see in the Holy Scripture and the tradition of the Church, is valid for all men. We can all attain deification.

We must make a constant effort to reach the catholic way of life, to experience the catholicity of the Church.

7

Orthodoxy and legalism

Orthodoxy and legalism

The Orthodox Church differs from other expressions and manifestations of Christianity at many points. I would not like to enumerate all the differences, but to point out one –that which is called legalism. We can say that the Orthodox Church, in contradistinction to other "Churches", is not characterised by legalism.

In what follows I shall try to analyse the topic of legalism, presenting at the same time the effects which the legalistic mind has on man's spiritual life and the fact that legalism really distorts the entire spiritual life.

There are probably some people who maintain that the Orthodox Church has elements of legalism. Those who support something of this sort are ignorant of true Orthodoxy and are confusing Orthodoxy with other traditions. In reality, the Orthodox Church is not conservative, but it is, first and foremost, traditional. And we know very well that there is a tremendous difference between tradition and conservatism. Conservatism retains the ossified forms of the past, estranged from life, while tradition, having life and experiencing it, conveys it in forms of the present. Thus it is by nature impossible to connect and identify the Orthodox Church with legalism, which does not presuppose the existence and living experience of the true life.

1. Antinomianism and legalism

First I must make the clear distinction between law and legalism. Law is the will of God and legalism is the living of the letter of the law, estranged from the spirit of the law. We shall establish all this difference in the following analyses.

Yet we must add that, unfortunately, today there are two unorthodox currents prevailing. We are committing two serious errors in the spiritual life which are corrupting the Tradition of the Church. One is antinomianism, that is to say, a rejection of God's Law for the sake of a wrongly understood freedom, the autonomous regulation of our life. And the other is legalism about the spiritual life, regulating our life on the basis of the letter of the Law because we have disconnected ourselves from the experience of the spirit of the Law[1]. Neither of these currents expresses genuine Christianity, because they set up erroneous and anti-orthodox views. And we can add that antinomianism is expressed chiefly by Protestantism, which has discarded and is discarding the laws and canons of the Church, the whole Tradition of the Church, for the sake of the "faith". And legalism about the spiritual life is expressed chiefly by Papism, which does not see the depth of the Law, as we shall see more analytically further on. Unfortunately, it must be added frankly that also some Orthodox have become steeped in these two currents, within the whole climate of influence which we have received from some western Christian Traditions.

I would like to mention a few examples in order to make

---

1. Archimandrite George Kapsanis: Pastoral ministry according to the holy Canons. Athos, Piraeus 1976, p.19 (in Greek)

clear these two anti-orthodox streams which prevail today and are influencing us, and to show how they differ from the genuine orthodox spirit and the true Orthodox Tradition.

One is fasting. Those who are characterised by antinomianism discard it with the justification that they are free and that it was legislated in later times in the Church. Those who are characterised by the spirit of legalism in the spiritual life keep the law outwardly, pharisaically, without applying and experiencing the whole atmosphere of the tradition of the Church. Fasting is intended to purify man, and for the nous to try to free itself from created things and material goods and to move towards God.

The second example is that of going to church, of our participation in the worship of the Church. The antinomians reject church-going, either altogether or in part, with the justification that God is everywhere present and therefore particular places of worship are not needed. Those who make the spiritual life legalistic on this point go to church but are not imbued with the atmosphere of worship, while not giving up the ecclesiastic tradition. Our participation in the divine Eucharist is inseparably connected with the experience of the deepest spirit of the divine Eucharist, which is self-emptying, the sacrificial way of life, offering, deepest humility.

And a third example is the kneeling which we do as a part of orthodox asceticism. Those who are possessed by antinomianism discard this way of asceticism, which they regard as a thing of the past, while those who are possessed by legalism keep this way of asceticism, but without having a personal connection. In the Orthodox Church the genuflexions and prostrations are connected with real and complete repentance, which is broken-heartedness.

They aim at the participation of the body as well in man's journey towards deification. It is taken for granted that the so-called hesychastic movement, which is the essence of orthodox theology, aims at the asceticism of the body as well, because it too will participate in the grace of deification.

These three examples show that in the Orthodox Church we do not accept either antinomianism or legalism in the spiritual life. We keep the Law, but we aim at finding and living the spirit of the Law, as we shall see, as our analysis of the subject continues.

2. Difference between Papism and Orthodoxy

I should like us to see the difference between Law and legalism, to analyse the difference between Orthodoxy and Papism. This is because in the Latin "Church" more legalism is experienced in both theology and life.

We should start with the distinction between organism and organisation. We say that the Church is not an organisation, but the Divine-human Organism. The organism is a living body, which means that it has life primarily. It can also be characterised by definite laws, but in the end it is life itself that comes first. The composition of an organisation becomes a basis for a legal process. That is to say, the legal composition comes first. We can see this difference between Orthodoxy and Papism. As has been pointed out characteristically, "for the westerners, God's relationship with man and the world could only be ethical and not one of grace and life. The sacraments, and especially the Divine Eucharist, Baptism and ordination become juridical means for salvation. The Church is reduced to a legal institution supplying salvation and created grace. In the establishment of the Church the legal institution comes before the sacramental composition. In Orthodoxy, on the contrary, the sacramental composition of the Church precedes, and the Church is protected and expressed through the Canonical institutions"[2].

In the West, and especially in the Latin "Church" there is a pronounced legalistic spirit in all the expressions. But what is terrible is that this legalistic spirit is fortified theologically as well, or I can add further that it is expressed by an erroneous theological position.

In what follows we shall look at this theological fortification of the legalistic spirit and its consequences for the spiritual life in Anselm of Canterbury's teaching about propitiation of divine justice, which is also a teaching of the Latin "Church"[3].

According to Anselm, God in His essence is love and justice. The sin which Adam committed, as well as every sin of man is an offense against God's justice. God's justice is offended by the committing of sin and, consequently, the demand for punishment is a necessity of the divine nature. From the way this is put, it seems that God is subject to some laws of necessity. Therefore he requires the satisfaction and propitation of His justice, which came about through the incarnation of Christ, the Second Person of the Holy Trinity, and His sacrifice on the Cross. Thus the purpose of the incarnation of the Word and His sacrifice on the Cross was the propitiation of divine justice, which was offended by man's sin.

---

2. Archimandrite George Kapsanis: Orthodox Tradition and Papism, Holy Mountain, 1979, p.12
3. See broader analysis in Protopriest John Romanides: "The ancestral sin, Pournara, 2nd ed., Thessaloniki 1970, p.87f.

This view is not valid from the orthodox point of view and can be characterised as heretical. In the holy Fathers we can find elements which refute this teaching of Anselm's. Some patristic views will be given.

God's justice and love are not His essence, but His energies. God is not love and justice in His essence and His nature, but in His energies, which are uncreated and are called essential or natural energies. We add further that God "is free of any necessity and any self-interest". It is sinful to ascribe to God the characteristic features of fallen man, such as that God is angry and vengeful and therefore He must be propitiated and appeased. Such an attitude wants to make it appear that it is God Who needs curing and not man. But this is sacrilegious. The sinful man who is characterised by egoism and arrogance is offended. We cannot say that God is offended. St. John Chrysostom says characteristically: "It is not He who is at enmity, but we; for God is never at enmity". We cannot say that God is man's enemy, but that man by the sin which he has committed, has become an enemy of God. Consequently, sin is not an offence of God, Who must be cured, but our own illness, and therefore we have need of a cure.

In any case, according to the holy Fathers no one can harm God. St. John Chrysostom points out: "No one will be able either to injure God with insults or make Him shine more brightly by praise, but He always remains in His appropriate glory, neither increased by praise nor decreased by blasphemy". Sin injures man and because of it our whole existence is ill. Nor do we add anything to God by doxology, but we ourselves are sanctified and share in His glory. Thus through Christ's incarnation and His sacrifice on the cross we have the restoration of man to his former glory and not a propitiation of God.

To be sure, there are expressions and terms in Holy Scripture which can be mistaken for propitiation of divine justice. One such term is 'reconciliation'. But if the sentences containing this word are interpreted in an orthodox and patristic way, we will discover that there is no meaning that God is reconciled by man, but that man is reconciled by God. The difference is very great and significant. Chrysostom observes: "Be reconciled to God. And he does not tell us to reconcile God to yourselves, for He is not the one at enmity, but we are; for God is never at enmity".

Thus by His sacrifice on the cross Christ did not propitiate His Father, but He cured the ailing nature of man. And this is said not solely about the sacrifice on the cross, but about the whole work of the divine Economy. The fact that He did not propitiate His Father, as is maintained by those in the West, is seen clearly in one remarkable passage in St. Gregory the Theologian. In his time there was discussion about the question, to whom Christ offered His blood, to the devil or to the Father. And St. Gregory answered that it is impious for us to maintain that God shed His blood and offered it as a ransom to the devil in order to release us from his domination. It is an "insult" for us to maintain that the devil received the blood of Christ. But neither did God need to receive the blood of His Onlybegotten Son, and therefore the Father did not need to be appeased by the blood of Christ. And St. Gregory asks: "On what principle did the Blood of His Only begotten Son delight the Father, Who would not even receive Isaac, when he was being offered by his father, but changed the sacrifice, putting a ram in the place of the human victim?". It is blasphemous for us to maintain that God the Father would be pleased to have the blood of His only begotten Son. What is unthinkable even on the human level is much

more unthinkable for God. And then St. Gregory says that
the Father neither asked nor needed the blood of His only
begotten Son. But Christ offered it in order to cure man
and to sanctify him.

At this point it must be made clear that there are some
who maintain that even from the orthodox point of view
we can speak of the satisfaction of divine justice, because
we also find such expressions in some holy Fathers. Characteristically he mentions St. Nektarios, who speaks of the
satisfaction of divine justice. In a book of his he is concerned with how Christ saved the human race. He writes:
"Being perfect man, having taken on the sin of the world,
and offering himself as a propitiatory sacrifice to His God
and Father, for the life and salvation of the world". And in
another place he says that Christ's incarnation was necessary and essential "because it had been proven that man of
himself could neither satisfy divine righteousness nor be
freed from the slavery of sin and the death which had entered through sin"[4]

Similar expressions which exist in several works of the
Fathers should be interpreted within the whole teaching of
the saints concerned and not piecemeal. Viewing and analysing the patristic passages piecemeal ends in heretical
deviations. They should also be studied from the point of
view of the so-called cataphatic theology. Specifically, with
regard to St. Nektarios, we should say that it does seem
that there is a verbal influence from the teaching of Anselm,
but there is an enormous difference. In the teaching of the
Latins the theory about propitiation of divine justice has

---

4. St. Nektarios: Orthodox Holy Catechism, ed. Rigopoulos, Thessaloniki 1972, p.71-72 (in Greek)

direct consequences in the spiritual life, because the whole ascetic effort is to cure God and not man, to satisfy God's justice, while in the teaching of St. Nektarios one can see the purpose of orthodox ascetic practice, which aims at man's cure. When one reads the letters which St. Nektarios sent to the nuns of the Holy Trinity of Aegina, he realises that the saint is an organic part of the whole neptic tradition of the Church, because he speaks about the illness of the nous, its cure, noetic prayer, purification of the heart, etc. Thus while it can be seen that there is a verbal influence, nevertheless this is clearly different from the ascetic teaching of the Latins.

This difference will be seen more in what follows, where we shall look at the extensions of the theory of propitiation of God's justice in life. As we have observed, this teaching does not remain theoretical, but it extends to all aspects of the spiritual life.

The Latins' whole effort is towards justifying themselves, appeasing God, and not towards their own cure. As has been observed, "a palpable example of the legalistic view of salvation is the way in which the sacrament of Repentance is practised by the Roman Catholics. Repentance and confession proceed like a lawsuit. The one being confessed tells his sins, separated from and unknown to the confessor (in the well-known wooden enclosure), and receives his penances and forgiveness. That is to say, there is no personal pastoral relationship and ecclesiastical communion, but a legal and impersonal relationship. The legal absolution of the sinner dominates, and not his forgiveness, return and restoration to the paternal home

---

5. George Kapsanis: Orthodox tradition... op. cit. p.12f

(the Church) and the paternal embrace"[5]. Likewise all the asceticism in the Latin tradition is aimed at man's being justified through satisfying God. There is a strong legalistic spirit. The penances, vows, journeys to the various shrines are a part of the atmosphere of man's absolution and the appeasement of God. Even the forgiveness of sins in the Latin tradition has a legalistic character.

In descriptions of men's daily life during the Middle Ages we see this whole legalistic view of the forgiveness of sins. The Clergy advised the people to travel to different shrines. In Rome among the objects which were worthy of being visited and seen by the pilgrims was the so-called "holy Shroud", on which was imprinted the face of Christ when, according to the tradition, they wiped Christ's sweat on His way to Golgotha. It was enough for the pilgrim just to see the Shroud in order to earn twelve thousand years of forgiveness of their sins (for the inhabitants of Rome it was only three thousand years)". Likewise, in a fourteenth century poem which had the title "the way of the Cross" is said that instead of going to Jerusalem and to Sinai, one can go to Rome. For if the various chapels in Rome were visited, they would receive forgiveness of their sins. In the same way, if people ascended the twenty-nine steps leading to the chapel in which the Apostle Paul celebrated the Divine Liturgy for the first time, they would receive forgiveness of their sins for many years. In this poem is said: "If you go there often, you will receive seven hundred years' forgiveness"[6]. Participation in the crusades also had the meaning of forgiveness of sins, among other aims.

---

6. Marjory Rowley: Daily life in the Middle Ages, ed. Papadima, Athens, 1988, p.119 (in Greek)

It is true that one can also observe such phenomena in the lay traditions of orthodox laymen. Even so, it must be recognised that there is an enormous difference. The legalistic tendency of the Latins stems from their theory about the appeasement of divine justice, from their theology about the ancestral sin and the guilt which men inherit. And not only does it stem from such erroneous positions, but it is a part of the whole climate of legalism which prevails in the Latin Church. While in Orthodoxy the admitted existence of some deviations has no bearing on the dogmatic truth of the Church, it does not stem from erroneous theological positions, but is due, on the one hand, to erroneous personal deviations, and on the other hand, to the immature condition of the Christian and his being influenced by other traditions. In the orthodox teaching we say that some belong to the state of the slave, others to the state of the hireling and others to the state of the son. In general, it must be pointed out that sin in the orthodox teaching is darkening of the nous, while repentance and forgiveness of sins are illumination of the nous. Sin is regarded as an illness of the soul. Sin is not placed in a legal framework, but a medical one.

In conclusion we can say that our relationship with God should not be regarded as juridical, legal, but as personal, ecclesiastical. The legalistic view is alien to the orthodox mind. When we think that God has been offended by the sin which we commit and that we must therefore do everything to appease Him, when our relationship with God is put on a business basis, then we are living in the legalistic spirit.

3. The value of the Law and the sacred Canons

From what has been said against legalism I do not want to create the impression that we are finding fault with God's Law and the sacred Canons or are ignoring their great value for our spiritual life. Moreover, in the beginning we made the distinction between Law and legalism. Legalism is to look at the surface of the Law without experiencing its essence and spirit. And we cited several examples to make this clear. In order for no erroneous impression to be created, I would like us now to look at the great value of the Law of God and of the sacred Canons of the Church. The will of God which aims at our salvation is expressed through the Law of God and the sacred Canons.

Through his creation by God and being placed in Paradise, Adam had personal communion with Him. The Law had not been given to him, apart from the commandment not to eat of "the tree of the knowledge of good and evil". According to the whole hermeneutical tradition of the Fathers of the Church, this prohibition had the character of preparing man and confirming him in the good, so that he should come to eating from the tree at a suitable time. And this, of course, would be his deification. Moreover, after his creation Adam was in the state of illumination of the nous, which is the first step of vision of God. Adam was in a state of seeing God and therefore there were not many laws and prohibitions.

But by his fall he fell into the darkening of his nous, with the result that he came to forget God. He lost his communion with God and instead of worshipping the real God he was worshipping idols. We know from the patristic teaching that forgetting God and not knowing Him are the greatest sins. Man became a pagan. Then God intervened out of love, and through His Prophets He gave the Law, so that man might distinguish between good and evil and thus acquire a safe guide on his journey towards true communion with God and gain true knowledge of Him.

With these preconditions the Law at first had a more negative character, it had prohibitory commandments, precisely because man was underdeveloped spiritually and had to learn to distinguish good from evil and make the distinction between uncreated and created energies. In spite of these things many men could not even keep even these commandments and therefore were looking for the coming of the Messiah to cure them. In this sense too we can see the fact that the Law was a teacher leading to Christ. Thus the coming of Christ brought life to man. It made it possible for him to attain personal communion with God, to eat His Flesh and drink His Blood and to have Christ dwelling in his heart. In this perspective we can use the saying of St. Gregory the Theologian, that by His incarnation Christ became man's unique and efficacious medicine.

St. Maximos the Confessor links the spiritual life with the existence and experiencing of the three Laws: the natural Law, or the conscience, the Law of the Old Testament and the Law of divine grace of the New Testament. And this link is not only temporal, historical, but also personal. After losing his pure conscience, which was to have led him safely on his journey towards God, man has need of the negative commandments, because at the beginning of our spiritual life we keep the negative commandments of Christ and after that we experience divine grace, which frees us from the dominion of sin. Thus the Law, Christ's commandments, the sacred Canons made by the Church, all have a therapeutic character. They cure man so that he may attain illumination and deification. Christ's commandments are a medicine which leads us to the cure. They presuppose the cure and lead man towards what is to be found there.

God's Law which is expressed through the commandments cures man. St. Philotheos of Sinai writes that "the divine and life-giving commandments" manifest God's all-holy will. And further, he says that God's commandments legislate for the three powers of the soul. As is known in the teachings of the holy Fathers, man's soul is divided into the intelligent, appetitive and incensive aspects. The devil attacks the three parts of the soul in various ways. And man cures his soul by keeping the commandments. St. Philotheos writes: "All the commandments of the Gospel seem to legislate for the tripartite soul and make it healthy through what they enjoin". They do not merely seem to make it healthy, "but they truly sanctify it". And then he cites many examples to show that God's Law, which is expressed through the commandments, actually cures man.

Of course when we say that God's Law cures man, it means that when a man is cured, then in fact the Law is transcended. The Law ceases to be external, the person ceases to struggle to apply it, and it becomes internal, the person's natural state. In the state of the vision of God and of deification man has personal communion with God and does not need to be reminded by any Law. St. Maximos says: "The effect of observing the commandments is to free from passion our conceptual images of things. The effect of spiritual reading and contemplation is to detach the nous from form and matter. It is this which gives rise to undistracted prayer". The commandments which refer chiefly to purification of the heart help the person to see the world without passion, that is to say without passions being mixed into the conceptual images of things. It is the vision of God, however, which detaches the nous from form and matter, frees it from every image and fantasy.

Thus the commandments, God's Law, are an essential therapeutic medicine for man to attain illumination and deification. However, in the state of the vision of God they are transcended, done away with. In the Kingdom of God after the Second Coming there will be neither laws nor commandments nor doctrines, because man will be participating in the deifying uncreated energy of God. The Apostle Paul is clear when he refers to this point: "Whether there are prophecies, they will fail; whether there are tongues, they will cease; whether there is knowledge, it will vanish away... But when that which is perfect has come, then that which is in part will be done away" (1 Cor. 13, 8-10). This passage refers not only to the life to come, but also to the present, when man reaches deification, as is seen also in what follows in the epistle: "now I know in part, but then I shall know just as I also am known" (1 Cor. 13, 12). According to the interpretation by Fr. John Romanides, this refers not only to the future, but also to the present life, to the state of the vision of God, vision of the uncreated Light. "In part" and "in a mirror dimly" refers to noetic prayer, while "face to face" and "I shall know as I am known" refer to the vision of the uncreated Light, which the Apostle had enjoyed and will enjoy also in the future. Furthermore, in the patristic tradition we are well aware that the last things are not just things awaited, but they are also present for the saints who share in the experience of deification.

Therefore in the experience of deification which is man's justification there is no Law, precisely because then the person has been cured. The Apostle Paul writes about the value of the Law and the overcoming of it: "But we know that the law is good if one uses it lawfully, knowing this: that the law is not made for a righteous person, but for the lawless and insubordinate..." (1 Tim. 1, 8-10). When a person has the Holy Spirit in his heart, he is experiencing justification and there are no problems about what the use of the Law requires. The Apostle is clear when he says "walk in the spirit and you will not fulfil the lust of the flesh" (Gal. 5, 16). To live and walk in the spirit means to have noetic prayer in one's heart, which is a sign that one's nous is illuminated.

Through the Law one recognises sin, that is to say, one can distinguish between the will of God and the will of the devil. Therefore the Apostle Paul says: "I would not have known sin except through the law" (Rom. 7, 7). But when a person attains the vision of God, then the Law is essentially done away with in the sense that the person is living in the atmosphere and purpose towards which the Law is directed. Then the Law becomes a natural condition and the prophecy holds true: "'Behold, the days are coming,' says the Lord, 'when I will make a new covenant with the house of Israel and with the house of Judah, not according to the covenant that I made with their fathers... For this is the covenant that I will make with the house of Israel after those days,' says the Lord. 'I will put my laws in their mind and write them on their hearts; and I will be their God, and they shall be my people'" (Heb. 8, 8-10).

It has been observed from church history that in the periods when the Christians had become secularised, many Canons were formulated, so that people could discern their spiritual instability, distinguish good from evil, and be guided on the path of the cure. So the law is not a human invention, but a revelation by God for man to be cured. Thus it is not a goal, but a means, a medicine necessary for man's cure. The wrong use of the Law, changing it from a means to an end, from a medicine to an ideology, is an unhealthy legalism, which constitutes the pharisaical justice and self-justification which do not save man.

4. Confession - penances

After this analysis we shall look at a practical subject. It is the subject of confession and in particular the subject of the so-called penances which we also have in the Orthodox Church.

We know that the holy Canons impose various penances for having committed various sins. They are chiefly imposed on people who are confessing and in some other necessary cases. But it is possible for us to set the penances in a legalistic spirit and then we distort them in an essential way. In other words, if we place the penances in an erroneous theological light as an appeasement of God, then we commit an error. In the Orthodox Tradition what are called penances do not have this meaning. They are not interpreted legally, but medically.

To look at the theological and orthodox view of the subject, we should say that the penances are closely connected with the theology of the Church with regard to sin and holy Communion. Since in the Orthodox Tradition sin is not an offence against God, but an illness, we can at once see the penances not as man's punishments or means of appeasing God, but as a medicine for our cure. And the Eucharist is not celebrated for sentimental reasons and moral improvement but for deifying man. But the holy Communion of the Precious Gifts works in a way corresponding to the spiritual condition of the person. If he is in the stage of purification, it helps him to be perfected and to reach illumination. If he is in the stage of illumination of the nous, then through Holy Communion God becomes illumination for him, and if he is in the stage of deification, then through Holy Communion God becomes deification and Light. Therefore, if the person has not entered the stage of purification, if he is not living in the state of repentance, then holy Communion becomes fire and Punishment. This appears in all the liturgical prayers in which we ask God that the Communion of the Precious Gifts may not be "unto judgement or unto condemnation". Just as the prohibition of some foods by the physician of our body does not mean a punishment, but presupposes the person's illness and is aimed at his cure, the same is also true of penances.

Like many of the holy Canons, Basil the Great divides sinners and penitents into different stages: they are the mourners, the listeners, the supplicants, the reconciled, and those partaking of the Sacraments. This division is from the point of view of curing the person, and not from the point of view of legal justification and appeasing God. So when someone is in a state of repentance on which Holy Communion will have a therapeutic and divine effect and not a punishing one, then he is permitted to receive communion. Therefore both the penitent and the Confessor should see the penances, the deprivation of Holy Communion, within this therapeutic and loving perspective. Otherwise the holy Canons are distorted, just as the Law of God is distorted in similar cases.

There are many patristic passages in which the therapeutic value and meaning of deprivation of holy Communion appears. Basil the Great, referring to sins which particular persons commit, and defining the way and time of repentance, says in the end epigrammatically: "We write all these things so that the fruits of repentance may be tested.

For in any case we do judge such things by the time, but we are careful about the way of repentance". The Synod of Neo-Caesarea, referring to various sins, says "Their mode of life and their faith shorten the time". The point is to cure the person. There is a characteristic saying of St. Gregory of Nyssa according to which depriving of Holy Communion someone who has been cured is just as improper as for the Confessor to give Holy Communion to someone who has not repented and has not been cured. St. Gregory of Nyssa writes epigrammatically: "For just as it is foolish to cast a pearl before swine, so it is unsuitable to deprive of the precious Pearl one who by dispassion and purity has already become a man".

The example which the Sayings of the Desert Fathers has preserved for us from the life and teachings of Abba Poemen is characteristic. "A brother questioned Abba Poemen saying: 'I have committed a great sin and I want to do penance for three years. 'The old man said to him, 'That is a lot. 'Those who were present said, 'For forty days?' He said again, 'That is a lot. 'He added, 'I myself say that if a man repents with his whole heart and does not intend to commit the sin and more, God will accept him after only three days'". The example shows that to be deprived of Holy Communion, the so-called penances, is a therapeutic medicine, it should be included in the therapeutic training of the Church.

In order to complete the subject, we can gather that the legalistic spirit, to look at the surface of the Law and keep some outward formal orders alienated from the whole ascetic, therapeutic atmosphere of the Church and linked with a juridical procedure, is a western concept and therefore does not belong to the orthodox mind. We must discard every juridical notion, every attempt to appease the divine justice. Let us first of all perceive sin as an illness of our nature, let us locate the illness in the darkness of the nous, at which time we will keep the Law in order to be cured, until we may attain deification, which is the deepest purpose of creation and of man's existence.

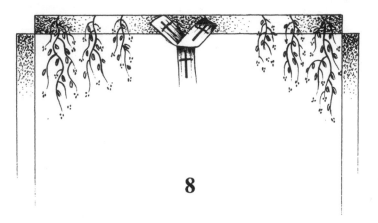

8

Secularism in the Church,
theology and pastoral care

Secularism in the Church, theology and pastoral care

I think that what we have said so far can give us some facts about what the Church is, what the reality of life is like and what the behaviour of the true members is like. In addition, we can help ourselves to make a comparison between the true and false way of life.

However, in the thoughts which follow I would like us to look at a crucial subject which needs to be confronted. It is the great issue of secularism in the Church, theology and pastoral care.

Secularism is the loss of the real life of the Church, the alienation of the members of the Church from the genuine mind of the Church. Secularism is the rejection of the ecclesiastical ethos and the pervasion of our life by the so-called worldly mind.

It must be said emphatically that the greatest danger is the secularisation of the members of the Church. The Church has many "enemies". But the worst and most dangerous is secularism, which is consuming the marrow of the Church. To be sure, the Church is not in any real danger, since it is the blessed Body of Christ, but the danger is for the members of the Church.

To be accurate, we would say that secularism, which consists in the adulteration of the way of life and the true faith, is connected with the passions and, of course, has been lurking in the Church from the beginning of its existence. Already in Paradise Adam tried to interpret God's commandment rationally. But even after Pentecost there were cases which manifested the Christians' anthropocentric way of thinking and living. The Gnostics and so many others are clear evidence of this.

But for the most part, secularism began after the cessation of the persecutions. During the persecutions, the Christians believed and lived in truth. But when Christianity became the official religion of the State, then the Christian faith and the way of life began to be adulterated. In reaction to this secularisation, there began to be anchorites, and then monasticism developed. In the early Church all the Christians lived monastically, as can be seen in Holy Scripture, especially in the Epistles of the holy Apostles. However, the coming of people into the Christian faith out of expediency resulted in secularisation of the Christian faith and the rise of monasticism. Monasticism is not something alien to the Church, but it is life according to the Gospel, which some Christians wanted to live in perfection and therefore decided on this way of life. It can be maintained that even the most eccentric monk is a healthy reaction to the secular spirit which is plaguing the Christians of our time.

Before we go on to look at how we are experiencing secularism in Church, theology and pastoral care, I would like us to examine more analytically what is the so-called secular mind, what we call 'world' in the Biblico-patristic tradition, because in any case the word for world (cosmos) is central in the word for secularism (ekkosmikeusis).

1. The double meaning of the word 'cosmos'

The word 'cosmos' in Holy Scripture and the works of the holy Fathers has two meanings. One is that cosmos is God's creation, the whole creation, and the other is that cosmos is the passions and what characterises the mind of flesh, which is deprived of the Holy Spirit.

First, cosmos is the creation. It is so called because it is an ornament, a jewel. In the Orthodox tradition we say that the world is a positive work of God. It is not a copy of another real world, the world of ideas, it is not a downfall from the real world, nor is it the creation of a lesser God. The phrase in the Creed –"I believe in one God, Father Almighty, maker of heaven and earth, and of all things visible and invisible"– was formulated in order to counter a teaching of certain ancient heretics that the world was created by a lesser God.

So the world is a creation of God. It is an ornament, a jewel. God created the world with His uncreated creative energy, because God creates with energy, not with essence. It is very characteristic that at the end of each creation the Holy Scripture notes: "and God saw that it was good".

God not only created the world, but He also maintains it with His providential energies. Christ's words which demonstrate God's love for the world are significant: "For God so loved the world that He gave His only begotten Son in order that whoever believes in Him should not perish but have everlasting life" (John 3, 16). This love of God for the world was expressed principally by the incarnation of Christ and the salvation of man. After all, man is the microcosm within the macrocosm and is the summing up of the whole creation.

The word 'world' in the sense of God's creation is found

in many places in Holy Scripture. John the Evangelist, speaking about Christ and about the incarnation of the Son and Word of God, says: "He was in the world, and the world was made through Him, and the world did not know Him" (John 1: 10). Likewise in many places it says that while the world was made by God, it can also be a deceit by the evil one, since it was through the world, through the creation, that the devil even deceived Adam in Paradise. Therefore the Lord says epigrammatically: "For what is a man profited if he gains the whole world, and loses his own soul?" (Matt. 16, 26).

The second meaning of the word 'world' is sin, the passions, the carnal mind, which is the mind deprived of the life and energy of the Holy Spirit. We find the word 'world' in this sense many times in Holy Scripture.

John the Evangelist, who frequently uses the word 'world' to denote God's creation, the entire creation, in other cases uses it also to denote the passions of the flesh, everything which draws man away from God, or man's life apart from God. The following is a characteristic passage: "Do not love the world or the things in the world. If anyone loves the world, the love of the Father is not in him. For all that is in the world - the lust of the flesh, the lust of the eyes, and the pride of life - is not of the Father but is of the world" (1 John 2, 15-16). John the Evangelist is not asking us not to love the creation, which God made, but the lust of the flesh, the lust of the eyes and the pride of life, which constitute in reality what is called the world.

In the Epistles of the Apostle Paul there is a characteristic passage showing that the world is, on the one hand, the desire of the eyes and the arrogance of life, all the external things that become the evil one's deceit and deceive us, and on the other hand, it is the passions of the soul, that is, the contrary-to-nature motion of the powers of the soul. The Apostle Paul says: "But God forbid that I should glory except in the cross of our Lord Jesus Christ, by whom the world has been crucified to me, and I to the world" (Gal. 6, 14). The Apostle is not boasting of his origins, of his Roman citizenship, of the fact that he saw Christ in His glory, but only of the Cross of Christ, through which he put the world to death. And this happened in a double way: First the world was crucified to him, then he was crucified to the world. In the first instance the devil could not deceive him by external incentives and in the second one the world of passions and desires which existed in him were completely eliminated.

It is in these two senses that we encounter the word 'world' also in the patristic texts. St. Gregory Palamas teaches that the world as created by God is neither to be held in contempt nor to be hated. In this meaning, the world has to be used by man for his maintenance. There is, however, a danger when someone views the world as a creature made by God and at the same time confronts it as the devil's deception, for the devil does indeed use the world to deceive man.

In Holy Scripture we read that the devil is ruler of the world. Interpreting this, St. Gregory Palamas says that the true ruler of the world is God, Who created it. The devil is called ruler of the world because he holds sway over the world of injustice and sin. In fact, "the abuse of beings, our passionate ruling over the world, the world of injustice, the wicked desire and arrogance...," this is the world whose ruler is the devil. It is clear that here the world means sin and passions.

Basil the Great, speaking of man's withdrawal from the world, says: "withdrawal from the world does not mean being bodily outside it, but withdrawal of the soul's sympathy towards it". Withdrawal is not flight from the world, it is not the soul's departure from the body, as the ancient philosophers said, but the soul's withdrawal of sympathy for the body. And of course when the Fathers speak of the body they do not mean the body in itself, but the mind of flesh, the passions of the flesh, worship of the body.

It is in this context that all the holy Fathers speak of the world. Theoleptos of Philadelphia says, "I call world the love of material things and of the flesh". He who is liberated from these "makes Christ his friend, possesses His love. And in general, to quote St. Isaac the Syrian, "when we want to name the passions collectively, we call them world".

It is in this sense that the word for world is used in the term for secularism and will be used in what follows. Secularism is the distortion of man by the mind of flesh and the passions. When our life is permeated with passions, with the world of injustice, and when we pursue this kind of life in the Church, in our thinking and theologising, it is secularism. In general, secularism is our life's estrangement from God, our not seeking communion and unity with Him, our attachment to the mundane and looking at everything and the issues in our life away from God's will. It could be said that secularism is a synonym for anthropocentrism.

What follows will be an analysis of the term 'secularism', of course in the broadest dimensions of the term.

2. Secularism in the life of the Church

We must emphasise from the start that when we speak of secularism in the Church, theology and pastoral care, we do not mean that the Church, theology and pastoral care are being secularised and destroyed, that the real life and the true method of man's cure are being lost, but that the members of the Church are being secularised and thus have a different view of the Church, theology and pastoral care. However, through the centuries there are members of the Church who preserve the truth about the Church, theology and orthodox pastoral care.

a) Secularism in the Church

We have already been given the opportunity to see what the term 'Church' means. Basically, we said that the Church is the Body of Christ. It is not a human organism, but the Divine-human Body of Christ. We also said that the Church is a communion of deification, which means that its aim is to guide its members to deification, which is the basic objective of man's creation.

There is a basic passage in the Apostle Paul's Epistle to the Christians of Ephesus which shows the objective of the Pastors of the Church. The Apostle writes: "And he himself gave some to be apostles and some pastors and teachers, for the equipping of the saints for the work of ministry, for the edifying of the body of Christ, till we all come to the unity of the faith and the knowledge of the Son of God, to a perfect man, to the measure of the stature of the fullness of Christ" (Eph. 4, 11-13). According to Nikodemos the Hagiorite, in the phrase "the knowledge of the Son of God", the Apostle Paul does not mean "the knowledge of God which is achieved through viewing created things and the Holy Scriptures; for the impure can also do this. He is speaking of the supranatural knowledge of the Son of God enhypostatised in the heart through divine illumination and glorification, which is given to many perfected who are purified of the bodily and physical passions something which he wishes all Christians to attain". Also the phrase "to the measure of the stature of the fullness of God" conveys the meaning of deification.

The existence of the true Church is demonstrated by its success in curing man. We know from the teaching of the holy Fathers that the Church is the spiritual health centre, the spiritual hospital that cures man. When we speak of illness and cure, we mean that the nous is ill and that it is cured. The cure of the nous is not independent of purification, illumination and deification. The aim of the Church is to cure this cognitive centre, so that man may attain the knowledge of God, which constitutes his salvation. Thus the existence of the true Church is shown by the degree of success, by the results of the therapy. If it cures man, if it diagnoses the illness correctly and if it knows the way and method of therapy, then it is the true, not the secular, Church.

However, there are some examples which show that the knowledge of therapy and success in curing is still going on in the particular Church. One of these examples is man's right social relationships. Actually, disturbed social and interpersonal relationships are a fruit and result of illness of the nous. The cure of the nous, which consists in its purification and illumination, also has sociological results. That is why things concerning the cure of the nous should be studied by what today is called the science of sociology. We Orthodox see the transformation of society in this light, and this is why we are realists. It is utopian for us to want to transform society by trying to find the suitable social system. It is not a question of a system, but of a way of life. This does not mean that we do not applaud every attempt to improve some bad conditions in the unstable and sick societies, most of which do not accept God's word. But the most effective and realistic way is through curing the nous.

The second example which shows the degree of a church's success in curing is the presence and existence of holy relics. The holy relics are a proof of man's cure. When the nous is purified and illuminated, and then when the man attains deification, then the whole man is deified, because the grace of God is transported from the soul to the body as well. The saints' relics, which are imperishable, fragrant and wonder-working, are a proof that the method and way of curing has been preserved, that the Church leads man to deification. Therefore it is said characteristically that the purpose of the Church is to lead man to deification. And a Church which does not produce relics shows that it is not leading man to deification, and therefore it does not have the true method for man to attain his cure.

The existence of the true Church can be recognised by the degree of its success. Just as in medical science we say that a sound medical theory is distinguished from an erroneous one by how successful it is, and just as a medical scientist is good according to how much he cures, the same can be said of the Church. An organised Church is one that cures man. Its existence is demonstrated by its success in curing the darkened nous.

Secularism in the Church is directly related to the loss of the Church's true objective. A Church that is not animated by what we have been saying, that is to say a Church that does not cure a man, but is occupied with other matters, is secular. It is in this sense that we can speak of secularism in the Church. Next we shall look at some cases illustrating the secularised Church.

We can say that the Church is secular when it is regarded as a religious organisation. There is an enormous difference between the Church and religion. Religion speaks of an impersonal God who dwells in heaven and directs the world from there. And man, by different rites and ceremonial acts, has to appease this God and come into contact with Him. But the Church is the Body of Christ, Who assumed human nature and in this way there exists a communion between man and God in the Person of Christ. To be sure, we do not deny that there are some Christians in the Church who have a religious sense of God. But this happens in the lower stages of the spiritual life, it constitutes spiritual immaturity, and nevertheless there is the disposition and tendency for man to go on maturing spiritually and to attain communion and unity with God. At all events, a secular Church simply satisfies people's religious feelings and nothing more. It is known for beautiful ceremonies and is unaware of the whole neptic and therapeutic wealth which the Church possesses.

Furthermore, the Church is secularised when it regards itself as a place and system of ideology, unrelated to life. Ideological systems are animated by abstract ideas and steeped in idealism, which bears the characteristic marks of all anthropocentric systems, which rest on philosophy and oppose materialism. Ideas are not much related to life, to the transformation of man. Idealism is put together by man's logic and is presented in the form of arguments and ideas.

The church does not function as an ideological field. It does not simply have some ideas, even if the best and most beautiful ones, which it can use to counter other ideas. The Church has life, and indeed the true life, which is a fruit of man's communion with God. St. Gregory Palamas says: "Every saying is countered by another saying". Every argument is confronted by a counter-argument. We see this clearly in so many philosophical ideas that have been formulated. But who can oppose the true life, and particularly the life which conquers death? The Church does not have ideas. It has the life, which is the transcendence of death.

It is a mistake, it is secularism, when we compare the Church with both the ancient and contemporary ideologies and with the contemporary ideological politico-economic systems. The Church does not simply copy the methods and ways of other social and philosophical systems, but it possesses a life which is beyond them, it has a different purpose which is not the same as that of the idealistic systems. To be sure, when the Church cures man, it also has great sociological consequences, but that is a result and fruit, never a cause and principle.

The secularised Church is occupied with human conjecture and abstract ideas. The real and true Church, however, does the same as true medicine, especially surgery. A surgeon can never engage in philosophy and culture or make conjectures while performing a surgical operation. He is faced with a sick man whom he wishes to cure, to whom he wants to offer health. In the same way the Church, faced with the sick man, can never indulge in conjectures and culture. The Church itself experiences the mystery of the Cross of Christ and helps man to experience it in his personal life. An experience of the mystery of the Cross is the deepest repentance, through which the nous is transformed from working unnaturally to moving in a natural and supranatural way.

Furthermore, the Church becomes secular when it is degraded into a social organisation like so many other organisations which exist in society. It is often said that the Church is the Nation's crowning institution. But the Church cannot be regarded as a national institution, even its crown. She can be the Nation's foundation, because the Nation's tradition is inextricably bound up with the tradition of the Church, and because the members of the Nation are at the same time members of the Church. However, the Church can never be institutionalised. When a revolution ends in bureaucracy, it loses its value, and this is its downfall. The same is true of the Church. The Church, which is the spiritual Hospital that cures man, can never be regarded as an institution supporting society and suitable for domesticating the citizens.

Unfortunately, some people today regard the Church as a necessary organisation, useful to society, and its role is valued according to its social usefulness. For many the Church is regarded as a forethought and the police as an afterthought, that is to say, the Church is fine for helping society, to avoid the need for police intervention. When the Church fails, the police step in. No one can exclude the benefit of the Church even in this area. A Christian who is cured does not bother the police and other repressive forces. But we cannot look at the presence of the Church only in this area, for then we have a secular Church.

Unfortunately, there are others too who do not see the prophetic and sanctifying role of the Church, which consists in the sanctification of man and of the whole world. Rather, they accept the Church only as an ornamental element. They need it as an ornament for various ceremonies and to brighten them with its presence. Or they consider that the presence of the Church is required to demonstrate broad social approval. But as it has been pointedly observed, not even atheists reject such a Church. I may add that such a secularised Church is the despair even of atheists. They can use it for the present, because it serves them, but when they too need the real presence of the Church in their lives, they will experience great disappointment.

Today there is a general tendency for us to regard the secular Church as the most useful for contemporary social needs. I can add that there is also a growing tendency for us to adapt the Church's preaching and teaching to these social needs, especially to the needs of a society which is functioning in an anthropocentric way, because we are afraid of being rejected. The Protestants and the Western "Churches" in general have succumbed to this temptation, and that is why they have spread much despair to those seeking therapy, who are longing to find the true Church to cure them.

In any case, a Church that crucifies instead of being crucified, that experiences worldly glory instead of the glory of the Cross, a Church that succumbs to Christ's three temptations in the wilderness instead of overcoming them, is a secularised Church. It is destined to help the fallen society to remain in its fallen state, and it spreads disappointment and despair to all who are trying to find something deeper and more essential.

b) Secularism in theology

Since theology is the voice and faith of the Church, this means that all that we have said about the Church so far also applies to theology. But we shall go on to say more about this particular subject and to look more analytically at how orthodox theology is being secularised.

Theology means 'the word about God'. But in order to speak about God, it is presupposed that one knows God. In the Orthodox Church we say that knowledge of God is not intellectual, but spiritual, that is to say it is connected with man's communion with God. In the teaching of St. Gregory Palamas, the vision of the uncreated Light is closely connected with the deification of man, with man's communion with God and with the knowledge of God. Therefore theology is identified with the vision of God and the theologian is identified with the one who sees God. One who speaks about God, even in conjectures, can also be called a theologian, and so the Fathers also give the name of theologian to the philosophers, but ultimately, from the orthodox point of view, a theologian is one who has seen the glory of God, or at least accepts the experience of those who have reached deification.

In this sense theologians are those who see God, those who have reached deification and received the Revelation of God. One such theologian is the Apostle Paul, who went up to the third heaven and many times describes and presents his apocalyptic experiences. This occurs to such an extent that St. John Chrysostom, speaking of the Apostle Paul and about the fact that in his epistles there are mysteries greater than there are in the Gospels, says that through the Apostle Paul "Christ said great and ineffable things, greater than through Himself".

The Apostle Paul, as he himself says in the third person, was caught up "to the third heaven" (2 Cor. 12, 2). I would like at this point to recall the interpretation by St. Maximos the Confessor, according to which the three heavens are in reality the three stages of the spiritual life. The first heaven is the end of practical philosophy, which is purification of the heart, expelling all thoughts from the heart. The second heaven is the natural vision of God, that is to say, the knowledge of the inner essences of beings, when a man is granted by the grace of God to know the essences of beings, to have inner unceasing prayer. And the third heaven is the vision of God, theology, through which one reaches, through the grace of God and through one's nous being caught up, as far as possible, to a knowledge of the mysteries of God and knows all the mysteries of the Kingdom of heaven. This is "the ignorance superior to knowledge", according to a characteristic saying of St. Isaac the Syrian. This ignorance, in relation to human knowledge, is the true knowledge of God. So this is how theology is the third heaven, which is a fruit and result of the purification of the heart and the illumination of the nous.

These things are related to another teaching of St. Maximos the Confessor according to which all appearances need to be crucified and all thoughts need to be buried. Then the word is resurrected in us, that is, the man rises to the vision of God and becomes a true theologian. This means that orthodox theology is closely connected with orthodox asceticism and cannot be understood apart from it.

In speaking about true theology, i think it is well also to recall what St. Niketas Stethatos said about the interpretation of Paradise. St. Niketas, who belongs organically to the whole Orthodox Tradition, thoroughly analyses how the Paradise which God had created in Eden is "the great field of practical philosophy". The tree of the knowledge of good and evil is the natural vision of God, and the tree of life is mystical theology. When man's nous is purified, then he can approach the tree of the knowledge of good and evil and from there attain the food of the tree of life, and acquire the gift of theology. All the holy Fathers pursued this path, and this is why they proved to be unerring theologians in the Church and the true Shepherds of the people of God. On the contrary, the heretics tried and still try to theologise in other ways, not through practical philosophy, the natural vision of God, and mystical theology, but with their impure hearts and conjecture. Therefore they failed and were expelled from the Church of Christ.

When theology is not a part of this framework, which all the holy Fathers presented, it is not orthodox, but secular theology. We find this secular theology in the West, because there they analyse and interpret Holy Scripture within their own human and impure conjectures, without the true presuppositions presented by the holy Fathers. Unfortunately, in some cases this has also influenced our own country.

A typical example of secular theology functioning outside the traditional patristic framework is what is so-called s c h o l a s t i c   t h e o l o g y , which was developed in the West between the eleventh and fifteenth centuries. It was named scholastic theology from the various schools which cultivated it. Its main feature was that it relied heavily on philosophy, especially that of Aristotle, and attempted to interpret everything about God by reason.

Scholastic theology tried to understand God's Revelation rationally and to harmonise theology with philosophy. It is characteristic that Anselm of Canterbury said: "I believe in order to understand". The scholastics first acknowledged God, and then by rational arguments and logical categories they attempted to prove God's existence. In the Orthodox Church, as it has been expressed by the holy Fathers, we say that the faith is God's Revelation to man. We accept the faith as we hear it, not so as to understand it afterwards, but in order that our hearts may be purified and we may arrive at the faith through seeing God and may ex-

perience the Revelation. Scholastic theology, however, accepted something first, and then struggled to understand it
through logical arguments.

Scholastic theology reached its highest peak in the person of Thomas Aquinas, who is regarded as a saint of the
Latin Church. He said that the Christian truths are divided
into natural and supernatural. The natural truths, such as
the truth of God's existence, can be proven philosophically, but the supernatural truths, such as the trinity of God,
the incarnation of the Word, the resurrection of bodies,
cannot be proven philosophically, but can be proven not to
be irrational. Scholasticism made a close link between
philosophy and theology, and especially with metaphysics. This resulted, on the one hand, in a distortion of the
faith, and on the other hand, in scholasticism itself falling
into complete disrepute, when the world image of metaphysics which prevailed in the West collapsed. Scholasticism is not blameless for this whole drama which exists in
the western world today on the subject of faith. The holy
Fathers teach that there is not natural and metaphysical,
but created and uncreated. The holy Fathers never accepted Aristotle's metaphysics, but this does not belong to the
present, so I shall not develop it further.

The scholastic theologians of the Middle Ages considered scholastic theology to be a development surpassing
the theology of the Fathers, and this was the starting-point
of the teaching of the Franks that scholastic theology is
higher than the theology of the holy Fathers. Therefore the
scholastics, who were concerned with reason, considered
themselves superior to the holy Fathers of the Church and
also considered human knowledge, which is a product of
reason, to be higher than Revelation and experience.

We should also see the conflict between St. Gregory Palamas and Barlaam in this light. Barlaam was essentially a scholastic theologian, who tried to take scholastic theology to the Orthodox East. His views that we cannot know exactly what the Holy Spirit is, thus ending in agnosticism; that the philosophers of ancient Greece were above the Prophets and Apostles, since reason is higher than the vision of God which the Apostles had; that the Light of the Transfiguration was something which happens and is finished, that the hesychastic way of life, that is to say, purification of the heart and unceasing noetic prayer, etc., is not essential, –all these are views of scholastic theology, which in reality constitutes a secularised theology. St. Gregory Palamas perceived this danger to Orthodoxy and with the power and energy of the Holy Spirit, and also with the experience which he himself had gained as a bearer and conveyer of the tradition of the holy Fathers, he confronted this great danger and preserved unadulterated the orthodox faith and the Orthodox Tradition.

Unfortunately, Barlaamism, which is an expression of the scholastic theology of the West and yet constitutes secularised theology, has passed into the orthodox East in other ways. And we notice that expressions of the contemporary ecclesiastical and theological life are animated by scholasticism, by Barlaamism. To be sure, there has recently been an attempt to cleanse our theology from its Babylonian captivity to the scholasticism of the West, a great effort is being made to release orthodox theology from the prison of scholastic theology that encircles it. But at the same time we must go on to experience orthodox theology, which is not a intellectual knowledge, but an experience, a life, it is closely connected with what is called hesychasm.

Secular theology, which is related to scholasticism, is

also expressed today in many ways. In what follows, I would like to mention some of them.

One is that we base our whole method of theology on reason and conjecture. We think about the orthodox faith, we rationalise the truths of the faith or we simply make a history of theology. We have almost reached the point of viewing theology as a philosophy about God, being unaware of the whole therapeutic method which our Church has.

Another way of experiencing Barlaamism and scholasticism is that we have limited theology to aesthetics. We have made it aesthetics. We can write many books and make great analyses concerning orthodox art, study the schools of hagiography, see the great value of Byzantine art, while scorning and overlooking asceticism, the hesychastic method, which is the foundation of every orthodox art. Purification, illumination and deification are the basis of all the arts and acts and sacraments of the Orthodox Church.

Another way is that we seek rebirth of the liturgical life of the Church without a parallel recovery and experience of the ascetic life of the Church. We speak of continual participation in the Sacraments without making a parallel effort to link this effort with the stages of spiritual perfection, which are purification, illumination and deification. We make great efforts for the people to understand the Divine Liturgy rationally, without making a parallel struggle for the experience of the spirit of orthodox Worship. We seek to abolish the iconostasis so that laymen can see what is going on, without examining the reason why the Church appointed the Iconostasis and the secret reading of the prayers. These things are not independent of the secularisation of the theology of the Church. The teaching of St. Maximos the Confessor and the historical research about this are very revealing. The catechumens cannot pray with the prayers of the faithful and the faithful cannot pray as the catechumens do. And if we study the teaching of St. Symeon the New Theologian about who the catechumens really are, then we shall be able to understand why the Church appointed the Iconostasis and the secret reading of prayers.

At all events, when our theology is not connected with the so-called hesychastic life, when it is not ascetic, then it is secular, it is scholastic theology, it is Barlaamist theology, even if we seem to be fighting Western theology and struggling to be orthodox.

c) Secularism in pastoral care

Pastoral care is not unrelated to the Church and theology, nor independent of them. Pastoral care is the work of the Church which aims at enrolling the person in her Body, making him a true member. Pastoral care is the Church's method for guiding man to deification. Besides, as we said before, this is the deepest objective of the Church. Furthermore, pastoral care is not independent of theology, since the real theologists are the real pastors, and those who shepherd in an orthodox way are doing this work theologically. This is why all that we have said about the Church and theology so far is also true of pastoral care.

The true Pastors of the Church are the deified, those who partake to various degrees in the deifying energy of God, or those who accept the deified and follow their teaching. So either we are deified or we will accept those who are, and will exercise pastoral care with their help.

Moses attained deification by grace, he saw God in His glory, and then took up the heavy task of the pastoral guidance of the people. And, as St. Gregory of Nyssa says, before seeing God, Moses was unable to separate two Hebrews who were exchanging blows, while after seeing God and receiving his mission from Him to do this work, Moses was able to guide such a difficult and stiff-necked people. It is characteristic that Moses passed all this experience of deification on to the people through his guidance and the laws.

This is to be seen in the whole life of the Church. St. Gregory the Theologian regards pastoral care as the most difficult science, and in any case he links it with the deification of man. Therefore he wants the Pastors to have been cured beforehand so that they can guide their spiritual children towards the cure and deification.

The sacred Canons of the Church present the pastoral method. If we examine the Canons as legal schemes and structures, we fail to see their true place within the Church. The sacred Canons, as we have said elsewhere, are medicines to cure man. A careful study of the Canons may lead us to the conclusion that they presuppose man's illness, which is the darkening of the nous, and they aim at man's health, which is the illumination of the nous and deification. According to Basil the Great, there are five stages for those who repent, namely: those who remain outside the Church, those who weep, those who are listening, those kneeling, those standing with the worshippers, and those communing of the Precious Gifts, the Body and Blood of Christ. These stages show that every sin, which constitutes darkening of the nous, is a repetition of the sin of Adam and a fall from the true life. Then a man ceases to be a living member of the Church of Christ. They also show that repentance is a man's struggle to become a member of the Church again.

We should also look at the existence of the Iconostasis in this light, as we said before. In former times there was no Iconostasis, but just a Veil, and all the people had visual communion with what was going on, because the whole Holy Temple was a place for the faithful, for the true members of the Church. There was a substantial space between the Narthex and the main part of the Temple. When someone had sinned, he could not be present in the Temple and pray with the faithful. Thus there was the class of mourners, who were essentially in the condition of the Catechumens. But later the secularisation of the faithful resulted in the penitents being allowed in the Temple, but the Iconostases had been put in place.

Of course, we are not concerned only with a few outward manifestations, such as the existence of the Iconostases. But I would like to emphasise that the pastoral concern of the Church and of the Pastors does not lie in any outward actions, in psychological rest and relaxation, but in the effort for the heart to be purified and the nous to be illuminated.

Unfortunately, today things are being done differently, and therefore we can speak of secularism in pastoral care. There is an attempt to use contemporary psychology, among other methods, in the pastoral guidance of people. Many are using the results of psychology to help people. To know a number of psychological methods as well is not such a bad thing. Yet I believe that if anyone who knows himself, and by the grace of God is watching all the movements of the passions within him, and indeed, is studying the books of Holy Scripture and the holy Fathers and is being guided by a deified Spiritual Father, he can acquire true knowledge of other men as well, because the problems of all men are essentially the same. But the use of contemporary psychology to guide men is a secular view of pastoral care and is bad for the following reasons.

It is a bad thing when nowadays asceticism and the he-

sychastic method which our Church has at its disposal is
being neglected. Usually we ignore the hesychastic tradition as it is expressed in ascetic writings like the Ladder of
St. John of Sinai. It is a pity for us to have and to ignore a
healthy tradition in our Church that aims not at psycho-
analysis but at psychosynthesis. For our souls are already
experiencing schizophrenia, fragmentation through being
scattered by the passions.

Likewise it is a bad thing when we maintain an anthropocentric position and think that man's health will improve
when we follow the method of listening and conversation.
Actually, the soul of man, who has been created by God
with the goal of attaining deification does not find rest
through moralistic advice and external human support. The
illness, as we said, is deeper, in the nous. It is not a matter of
certain suppressed and traumatic experiences of the past,
but of the darkening and deadening of the nous. The cure of
the nous and its illumination cannot happen through anthropocentric methods, through advice and psychoanalyses.

What is more, the use of contemporary psychology creates problems, because it is already considered to be a failure, even in the West. Many people have discovered that
psychology cannot cure man effectively. This can be seen
in two cases. One is that in the West there has also been
developed a so-called "anti-psychiatry", which strongly
opposes psychiatry because it has understood that it is on
an erroneous path, since it has set different assumptions
about the illness. Anti-psychiatry regards classical psychiatry as a form of social violence perpetrated on man. The
other case is that even the psychiatrists themselves understand the failure of psychology and psychiatry to cure,
because they are gradually abandoning psychiatry and turn-
ing more to neurology, since it is believed that many pro-

blems arise from man's neurological system, which has its centre in the brain. They say that many psychological abnormalities, such as illusions, hallucinations, and so on, have their origin in the illness of brain centres. Unfortunately in Greece all the new scientific discoveries come thirty to fifty years later.

In conclusion we can say that secularism is the greatest danger for the Church. It is this which adulterates her true spirit, her true atmosphere. Of course, we must repeat that it does not adulterate the Church, but the members of the Church, because the Church is the true and sanctified Body of Christ. Therefore we should rather speak of the secularisation of the members of the Church.

The Church is the Jewel of the world, the mercy of mankind. But when this jewel of the world is permeated by the so-called secular spirit, when the Christians, the members of the Church, instead of belonging to this jewel and instead of being the light of the world, are permeated by the world in the sense of the passions, and become world, then they experience secularism. And this secularism does not lead to deification. It is an anthropocentric view of our life. The Church should enter the world in order to make it become Church, not the world enter the Church and make it become world.

A secularised Church is utterly unfit and unable to make the world become Church. And the secularised Christians have failed on all levels.

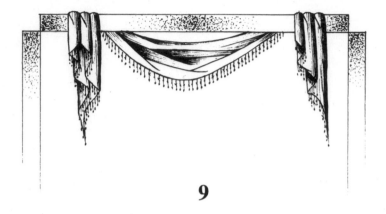

9

The "Synodikon of Orthodoxy"

The "Synodikon of Orthodoxy"

The "Synodikon of Orthodoxy" is a text contained in the "Triodion" and read on the Sunday of Orthodoxy, the first Sunday of Lent.

It is well known that through the ages various heresies have appeared which deny the experience of revelation and in fact make use of philosophy and conjecture, doubting the Church's truth on various dogmatic topics. The Fathers who formed the Synods opposed these errors. The decisions of the Synods on dogmatic topics are called "provisions". More generally speaking, each decision of the Synods is called a "Synodikon". Thus we have the synodical tome and the synodical provision, and moreover, each synod has its own synodikon.

The "Synodikon of Orthodoxy" is the decisions of the Seventh Ecumenical Council, which refer to the veneration of holy icons. The reading of them on the Sunday of Orthodoxy gave the title "Synodikon of Orthodoxy". Of course it must be said that later there was also added to the "Synodikon of Orthodoxy" the definition of faith of the hesychastic Councils of the fourteenth century. Thus the "Synodikon of Orthodoxy" comprises the decisions of both the Seventh Ecumenical Council and the Councils of the fourteenth century, which, as will be said below, have all the elements to characterise and regard as a Ninth Ecumenical Council.

An analysis will be made of the "Synod of Orthodoxy" in its central points. There will not be a broader analysis of the whole Council, but what I consider to be the main points will be emphasised, because they express the ethos of the Church. And this is necessary, because the mind of the Church is linked to, and in harmony with the decisions of the Fathers of the Church as it has been expressed with conciliar authority.

l. Church and Synods

However, before proceeding to analyse the "Synodikon of Orthodoxy", I think it well to examine briefly the large subject of the relationship of the Church with the Synod.

When some heresy springs up, the holy Fathers confront it at the place where it appears. Arios, who proclaimed that Christ is the first creature of God and essentially denied the divinity of Christ, was confronted by the Council of Alexandria. But then, when his heretical opinions began to be disseminated beyond the borders of Alexandria as well, the subject was confronted by the First Ecumenical Council. The holy Fathers were called together to make a common decision about the formulation of the orthodox teaching. In the Councils the holy Fathers did not seek to find the truth, making conjectures by reasoning and imagination, but in order to confront the heretics they attempted to formulate in words the already existing revealed Truth, of which they also had their own personal experience.

St. Nikodemos the Hagiorite divides the Councils into Ecumenical, Local and Rural. This division is not according to subjects, but according to the persons who brought them together, for it is possible that the subjects of the Local Councils can refer to serious dogmatic questions.

A Rural Council is a meeting which is convoked by the Bishop, Metropolitan or Patriarch alone with his own Clergy, without the presence of other Bishops.

A Local Council is a meeting in which the Metropolitan or Patriarch joins with his own Bishops or Metropolitans. This takes place when the Bishop of a district or the Bishops of two districts come together to confront various burning questions of the Church[1].

An Ecumenical Council is the assembly of many Bishops from all districts in order to discuss and decide about a question of the Church. The Ecumenical Council has four distinguishing marks according to St. Nikodemos the Hagiorite. The first is that it is convened "by order, not of the Pope nor of such and such a Patriarch, but by Royal orders". The second is that there should be discussion of topics of faith "and afterwards a decision and a dogmatic definition should be published in each one of the Patriarchates". The third is that the dogmas must be correct in their orthodoxy and in agreement with the divine Scriptures, or the previous Ecumenical councils". The words of Maximos the Confessor are characteristic: "The right faith validates the meetings that have taken place, and again, the correctness of the dogmas judges the meetings". And the fourth is that it must have universal recognition. All the orthodox Patriarchs and Archbishops of the catholic Church must "agree and accept the decisions and canonisings by the Ecumenical Councils, either through their personal presence or

---

1. Nikodemos the Hagiorite: Pedalion, ed. Papadimitriou, p.366, note 2 (in Greek)

through their own delegates, and in their absence, through their letters"[2].

These characteristic marks mentioned by St. Nikodemos the Hagiorite are noteworthy. But I must clarify two of them, the first and fourth, which are those most characteristic of the Ecumenical Councils and distinguish them from the other, Local Councils.

One is that the Ecumenical council was convened by the emperors, when Christianity had become an official religion of the Empire, and the emperor wanted to make the definition of the Ecumenical Council a law of the Empire for the peace of the Citizens. Fr. George Florovsky observes: "In a certain sense the General Councils as inaugurated at Nicaea, may be described as "Imperial Councils", die Reichskonzile, and this was probably the first and original meaning of the term 'Ecumenical', as applied to the Councils"[3].

The other was that the authenticity of the Ecumenical Councils as well as that of the other Councils was given chiefly by the deified and god-bearing Fathers. Fr. George Florovsky observes also at this point: "the ultimate authority —and the ability to discern the truth in faith— is vested in the Church which is indeed a 'Divine institution' in the proper and strict sense of the word, whereas no Council and no 'Conciliar institution' is 'de jure divino', except in so far as it happens to be a true image or manifestation of the Church herself". Then he says: "The claims of the Councils were be accepted or rejected in the Church not on formal or 'canonical' grounds. And the verdict of the Church has been

---

2. op. cit. p. 118, note 2
3. George Florovsky: Bible, Church, Tradition, p. 95

highly selective. The Council is not above the Church, this was the attitude of the ancient Church"[4].

In the foregoing chapters we explained in brief who are the true members of the Church, who are the living and who the dead members of the Church. So we can say that the mind of the Church is expressed by its deified saints. Therefore, finally, all the Ecumenical Councils rest upon the teaching of the saints of the past. The reader can find this view developed in an earlier study of mine[5]. Here I want only to mention George Florovsky's opinion that "both a few and solitary confessors of the faith were able to express this experience, and this is enough... the holy worthiness of the meeting does not depend on the number of members who represent their church. A great "general" synod would be able to be proven a synod of thieves (latrocinium) or even of apostates... But it is possible in a synod for the minority to express the truth. And most significant, the truth could be revealed even without a synod. The opinions of the Fathers and ecumenical Teachers of the Church often have greater spiritual value and explicitness than the definite decisions of synods. These opinions are not necessary to confirm and to be demonstrated by "ecumenical agreement"[6].

Likewise, I would also like to mention the opinion of Fr. John Romanides, that all the holy Fathers followed the same method and had personal experience of the truths of the Faith. Their meeting in an Ecumenical Council gave them the opportunity to agree on the same terminology for

---

4. op. cit. p. 97
5. See Archim. Hierotheos Vlachos: The Revelation of God, Monastery of the Birth of the Theotokos, 1987, p. 43ff
6. George Florovsky: op. cit. p. 72-73

the same revealed experience. He writes characteristically: "Neither illumination nor glorification can be institutionalised. The sameness of this experience of illumination and glorification among those having the gifts of grace, who have these states, does not necessarily require sameness of dogmatic expression, especially when those gifted are geographically far apart over long periods of time. In any case when they meet, they easily agree about the same form of dogmatic formulation of their identical experiences. A great impetus towards identical dogmatic expression was given at the time when Christianity became an official religion of the Roman Empire and satisfied the Empire's need to distinguish the genuine healers from the pseudo-physicians, in the same way in which the governing officials are responsible for distinguishing genuine members of the medical profession from the quacks and embezzlers of medical science, for the protection of their citizens"[7].

With these basic preconditions the Ecumenical Councils are unerring and express the consciousness and the life of the Church. And of course the terms of the Ecumenical Councils have value, because, on the one hand, they assure the possibility of salvation, and on the other hand they indicate the true way for man's cure, for attaining deification. We can say that the terms of the Ecumenical Councils are not philosophical nor do they serve philosophy, but they are theological, that is to say therapeutic, and they aim at the cure of man. Therefore we owe great thanks to the Fathers who formed the Ecumenical Councils and acted as ecclesiastic personalities.

---

7. Protopriest John Romanides: Jesus Christ the life of the world, multigraphed talk, Greek translation, p. 59

2. The two Ecumenical Councils

In the "Synodikon of Orthodoxy" there is reference to all the Fathers who formed the Ecumenical Councils, but mainly it was limited to mentioning and referring to two Councils with great authority and great authenticity. They are the Seventh Ecumenical Council, which ruled about the veneration of the holy icons, and the one taken to be the Ninth Ecumenical Council, which ruled about the uncreated essence and the uncreated energy of God, as well as ruling in an inspired way about hesychasm, the way which we should use in order to reach deification.

The Seventh Ecumenical Council was convoked by the grace of God, and the "decree of the devout and God-loving sovereigns Constantine and Irene, his mother", as it is said in the definition of faith of this Council. Indeed it is said that "the Lord God in His good will convoked us the leaders of the priesthood everywhere, with the divine zeal and consent of Constantine and Irene, our most faithful sovereigns". They contrast themselves with the heretics who, while said to be priests, in reality are not", for they have made accusation against the true faith of the Church "following impious men of the same persuasions".

Many things appear in this text. First, that the Ecumenical Council is convened in the name of the Imperial Sovereigns. Secondly, that the heretics, while they are priests, are really not, since the apostolic succession is not only the uninterrupted priesthood, but also adherence to the apostolic tradition and teaching. Thirdly, that the heretics repudiate the catholic teaching of the Church and follow philosophers, who have their own opinions and conceptions.

Appearing in the "definition of faith" of the Seventh

Ecumenical Council is the orthodox teaching about veneration of the holy icons, because "honour paid to the image passes on to the original" and "he who venerates the image is venerating in it the person of him who is depicted therein"[8].

In the "Synodikon of Orthodoxy" the whole faith of the Church concerning the veneration of the holy icons is conserved. The possibility of painting an icon of Christ is proclaimed precisely because he became incarnate and assumed human nature in fact, not in imagination. In the person of the Word the divine nature was united with the human nature immutably, unchangeably, inseparably and indivisibly. That is confessed which is different in essences and was united in this way in the one hypostasis of the Logos "the created and the uncreated, the visible and the invisible, the passible and the impassible, the limited and the unlimited". To the divine essence belongs the uncreated, the invisible, the impassible and the unlimited, while to the human essence belongs, apart from the other things, also the circumscribed. For this reason we can make icons of Christ, because He became incarnate. Anyone who does not tolerate "icon painting of the incarnate Word, and His sufferings on our behalf" is anathematised.

Also, in the "Synodikon of Orthodoxy" it is proclaimed that by bowing before the holy icons and by looking at them, the eyes too are sanctified and the nous is lifted up towards the knowledge of God. It is written characteristically: "the lips of those sanctifying by the word, or the ears by the word of those knowing and proclaiming, just as the eyes of those who see are sanctified by the pure

---

8. Fr. John Romanides: Texts of dogmatic and symbolic theology of the Orthodox Catholic Church, ed. Pournara 1972, p. 141-144

Icons, the nous is lifted up by them towards knowledge of God, just as also by the divine temples and holy implements and other precious vessels".

Thus we have the possibility to venerate the flesh of God and to be sanctified by this veneration, naturally according to the condition in which we are, since the flesh of Christ is characterised as "equal to God and of equal worth".

The Ninth Ecumenical Council in the time of St. Gregory Palamas was concerned with another doctrinal topic, which is a sequel to the topics that concerned the early Church. In the fourth century the holy Fathers confronted the heresy of Areios, who taught that the Word of God is a creature. St. Gregory Palamas in his time confronted the heresy of Barlaam, who said that God's energy is created. Furthermore, as we said, the Council "justified" hesychasm, which is the only method that leads man to deification. We must say that everything in the Ninth Ecumenical Council has all the elements and hallmarks which we cited above to qualify it as an Ecumenical Council.

First, it is convoked by emperors. In the synodical tome of 1341 A.D. it is said, among other things: "Then when the meeting had gathered, also in the presence of the eternal and blessed ruler... of the convocation and not a few of the most worthy archimandrites and abbots and assembled members of the government...".[9]. All three Councils which were convoked in this period on the doctrinal topic which was concerning the Church at that time, were convoked by order and in the presence of the emperors.

Then, as we said before, the subject of the uncreated energy of God, as well as what was called hesychasm were serious theological questions. That is to say, they are not

---

9. ibid. p. 236

subjects that refer to a few canonistic questions, but serious dogmatic themes that refer to man's salvation. For if
God's energy is created, then we end either in agnosticism
or pantheism. We cannot attain communion with God. And
if hesychasm, the way of the orthodox tradition by which
we are cured and attain deification, is replaced by philosophy, this too destroys the true preconditions for man's
salvation. Therefore these subjects are most serious.

Many contemporary theologians believe that the Councils of St. Gregory Palamas's time should be considered to
constitute and compose the Ninth Ecumenical Council. And
this is because they were called together by the emperors,
were concerned with a doctrinal topic of great importance,
and St. Gregory Palamas, who has attained deification and
therefore had personal experience of deification, was bat-
tling in them. I would like to refer to the opinion of Father
Athanasios Gievtits, who says: "But we think that the Council of Constantinople at the time of St. Gregory Palamas in
1351, judging at least from its great theological work, can
be, and deserves to be counted among the Ecumenical
Councils of the Orthodox Church, lacking in nothing as to
the soteriological significance of its theology. This Council constitutes the proof of the conciliarity of the Orthodox
Church and of the living experience and theology concerning salvation in Christ"[10].

This is also the conscience of the Church. That is why
in the "Synodikon of Orthodoxy" which existed already
and was read in the Churches, about the victory and triumph of the Orthodox, they added also "the chapters against
Barlaam and Akindynos", from what is called the Ninth

---

10. Hieromonk Athanasios Gievtits: Christ, beginning and end, ed. Gou-
    landi-Chorn, p. 195

Ecumenical Council. Emperor Kantakuzinos, at the last Council which was concerned with this topic, that is to say in the Council of 1351 A.D., summarised the conclusions of the meetings and decisions, while St. Philotheos Kokkinos, then Metropolitan of Heraklia, assisted by George Galisiotis and the wise Maximos put together the synodical tome from the records. Finally, the hesychastic teaching entered into the "Synodikon of Orthodoxy" for the first time, on the Sunday of Orthodoxy in 1352 A.D. in order for the heretics to be anathematised and all who expressed the orthodox teaching to be acclaimed. After the death of St. Gregory Palamas acclaim for him was added[11].

3. Anathemas - Acclamations

Anyone who reads the "Synodikon of Orthodoxy" will discover at once that, on the one hand, the heretics are anathematised and on the other hand the holy Fathers and confessors are acclaimed. For the former those present proclaim "anathema" three times, for the latter the people proclaim "eternal memory" three times at each proposal.

Some people are scandalised when they see and hear such action, particularly when they hear "anathema". They consider it very harsh and say that the spirit of hatred of other doctrines which the Orthodox Church has is being expressed in this way.

But the facts are not interpreted in this way. The anathemas cannot be regarded as philosophical ideas and as states of hatred for other doctrines, but as medical actions. First of all the heretics by the choice which they have made

---

11. Gregory Palamas: Syggrammata, ed. Panag. Christou, Thessaloniki 1988, vol. 4, p. 41-43 (Gk)

have ended in heresy and in their departing from the teaching of the Church. By using philosophy they have opposed themselves to theology and the Revelation. In this way they demonstrate that they are ill and in reality are cut off from the Church. Then excommunication has the meaning of showing the separation of the heretic from the Church. The holy Fathers by this action of theirs confirm the already existing condition, and besides this, they help the Christians to protect themselves from the heresy-illness.

There is a characteristic extract from the records of the Fourth congress of the Seventh Ecumenical Council. It says there that the holy Fathers fulfil the word of Christ, in order to set the lamp of divine knowledge "on the lampstand" to shine on all those in the house and not to hide it from them "under a bushel". In this way those who confess the Lord are helped to travel unimpeded the path of salvation. The holy Fathers "push away every error of heretics, and if the rotten limb is incurable they cut it off; and possessing the shovel, they cleanse the threshing-floor; and the grain, or the nourishing word, that which supports the heart of man, they store up in the warehouse of the Catholic Church, but the chaff of the heretical wrong teaching they throw out and burn in unquenchable fire"[12].

Thus the heretics are incurably rotten limbs of the Church and are therefore cut off from the Body of the Church. The heretics must be examined in this light. In this way one can see the Church's love for mankind. For, as we have emphasised elsewhere as well, when someone employs erroneous medical teaching, there are no therapeutic results, one can never achieve the cure. The same is true with the doctrines or the erroneous teaching. An erro-

---

12. Fr. John Romanides: op. cit. p. 147

neous teaching which is based on a wrong methodology can never lead man to deification.

It is in this light that we must examine the fact that the anathemas as well as the acclamations are referred to particular persons, because these particular persons are the ones who shape these teachings and as a result win adherents. And indeed it is characteristic that dreadful epithets are used for the heretics. We must add that the awful epithets which are used must not be examined in a moral sense, but in a theological sense, for many of the leaders of heresies were "moral" men. In what follows I would like to look at a few such epithets and some very indicative characterisations.

The iconoclasts who inveighed against the holy icons are called in the "Synodikon of Orthodoxy" "damaging" to the glory of God, "venturers against the icon and insolent, cowardly and fleeing". Those who started the heresy of iconoclasm, in the time of the Isaurians were called "sacrilegious and leaders of perdition". The Gerontios is anathematised for "the poison of its abominable heresy... with its perverse dogmas". Heresy is an illness and the heretical dogmatic belief is perverse, because it twists the truth of the revelation of the Church. Anathema is given to "the raging gathering against the venerable Icons".

As we said, all the heretics are mentioned in the "Synodikon of Orthodoxy". By this it seems, on the one hand, that all the heretics used the same method and in essence coincide with one another, and on the other hand, that both the Seventh Ecumenical Council and what is taken to be the Ninth Ecumenical Council regard themselves as expressing the Church and as a continuation of the earlier Ecumenical Councils. Arios is called a fighter against God and ringleader of the heresies, Peter the Purifier is called mad. The same characterisation "mad" is used of many heretics. Of course they are called mad not in a biological sense, but first and foremost in the theological sense. Barlaam, Akindynos, leaders of the anti-hesychastic teachings and all their followers are called an evil gang. By contrast, for the defenders of the orthodox teachings such adjectives as devout, most holy, and unforgettable are used.

And again I must point out that heresy reverses the true way of man's cure for reaching deification. If we think that purification of the heart, illumination of the nous is therapy in order for man to take the path to deification, then we understand that heresy reverses this way and leaves man permanently without a cure, without hope of cure and salvation.

4. Some characteristic signs

Of course it is impossible for us to analyse and interpret the whole wonderful and significant of the "Synodikon of Orthodoxy". The reader should go through it carefully and he will discover its importance. But I would like to have us look at some characteristic points which I think are the basis of all that is said in the "Synodikon of Orthodoxy" but also the basis of the Christian life, and which are the things that show to what extent we possess the genuine mind of the Church.

a) The condemnation of philosophy

In the whole text of the "Synodikon of Orthodoxy" it is seen clearly that philosophy is condemned. Both the way in which philosophy refers to and presents God and the conclusions to which it comes are condemned. And of course, in speaking of philosophy, we mean metaphysics as it was developed by Plato, Aristotle and other, later philosophers. We shall see what kinds of heretical teachings are cast out and rejected.

Those are rejected which accept the impious dogmas of the Greeks, that is to say the idolatrous ones, which refer to the creation of the world and to human souls and mix them up with the teaching of the Church. Characteristically it is said: "To those who have promised to revere the Orthodox and Catholic Church, and instead disgracefully introduce the irreverent dogmas of the Greeks about men's souls, and heaven, and earth, and the other created things, anathema". It should be pointed out that those who accept the dogmas of the Greeks but present themselves as devout are anathematised. It seems that also at that time there were men who, among other things, feigned reverence and had fine manners but did not accept the dogmatic teaching of the Church.

Yet it is not these works of the philosophers that are anathematised, but the fact that the teachings of the philosophers are preferred to the Faith, and that philosophy is used to distort the truth of the Church. It is not forbidden to study the works of the ancient Greeks, that is, of the pagans, but those Christians are reproached who follow and accept their futile theories. Anathema is pronounced "on those who accept the Greek teachings, not on those who only cultivate them for culture, but on those who also follow these futile doctrines of theirs". And as we said before, those are censured who prefer "the foolish so-called wisdom of the profane philosophers" to the orthodox teaching.

The "Synodikon of Orthodoxy" does not stay on a theoretical plane but also proceeds to concrete topics which it condemns. And, as will be discovered, it refers to basic teachings of philosophy, of so-called metaphysics. Among these is Plato's teaching about ideas. According to this notion, there are the ideas, and the whole world is either a copy of these ideas or a fall from these ideas. According to Plato, man's salvation lies in the return of his soul to the world of the ideas. In the "Synodikon of Orthodoxy" the holy Fathers condemn this view and those who accept "the Platonic ideas as true".

The ancient philosophers believed that matter has no beginning and all created things are everlasting and without beginning, and indeed matter is as old as the Creator of the world. Those who accepted these things are condemned. Matter and the world were created by God and do not remain unchangeable.

But also on the subject of creation philosophy differs from theology. It is a basic teaching of the Fathers of the Church that the world was created out of nothing, "out of non-being", out of "non-existent matter". This teaching shakes all the foundations of philosophy. Philosophy believes, as we said, that matter is everlasting. So those who accept that "all things did not come into being from non-being" are condemned by the "Synodikon of Orthodoxy".

Philosophy also differs on the subject of the soul, and therefore all who accept its views are condemned. The ancient philosophers believed in the pre-existence of the soul, in transmigrations and in the fact that the soul has an end, that at some time the soul will die. Such teachings have also entered into some theologians of the Church, and so they too are condemned. All are anathematised who accept "that souls have pre-existence" as well as all who accept "the transmigration of human souls, or even that they are destroyed by dumb animals, which are received into nonbeing", and therefore they deny "resurrection, judgement, and the final reward for the conduct of their lives". Likewise all those are condemned who assert that men will be raised with other bodies and will not be judged "with them according to how they conducted themselves in the present life".

Correspondingly, also those are condemned who accept the belief of the philosophers that there will be a restoration of all things, that is to say, "that there is an end to hell or a restoration again of creation, and of human affairs".

As there are even today, so there were then as well, men who considered the philosophers to be superior to the Fathers of the Church and therefore accepted their teachings. However, all are anathematised who teach that the philosophers, who were condemned by all the Ecumenical Councils, "are much greater, both here and in the judgement to come, than the holy Fathers, all who reject the teachings of the holy Fathers and the acts of the Ecumenical Councils, and all who do not take the teachings of the holy Fathers to be correct and try to "misinterpret them and turn them round" - all these are anathematised. For the holy Fathers are bearers of the Tradition, they are inspired by the Holy Spirit.

We mentioned before that all the philosophers had a particular method which they distinguished from the methodology of the holy Fathers. The philosophers used logic and imagination to interpret these things, while the holy Fathers attained illumination of the nous and deification, and in this way received the Revelation. The erroneous method of the philosophers as well as those who use it are condemned by the "Synodikon of Orthodoxy". By contrast, there is praise for pure faith and the simple and whole heart. Concretely, it says: " To those who do not accept with a pure faith and a simple and whole heart that which concerns our Saviour and God and our pure Theotokos who gave birth to Him, and who do not accept the remarkable miracles of the other saints, but who, attempting by proofs and sophisticated words, to defame them as impossible or to misinterpret them according to how it seems to them, giving advice according to their own opinion, anathema". When someone relies only on logic and imagination, he is on a wrong path. And if we observe carefully, we shall discover that all the heretics take this way. They try, through logic and imagination and by the use of philosophy, to analyse and understand all the doctrines of the Church. By contrast, the holy Fathers use a different method, which is called hesychasm, consisting of purification of the heart, illumination of the nous and deification.

In saying all these things we must again emphasise that the philosophers in their time made a great attempt to interpret some problems that they were trying to solve. But what we can observe is that they employed a different method and therefore fell wide of the mark. By the things said in the "Synodikon of Orthodoxy", we are urged not to cease studying the writings of the philosophers and the ancient Greeks, but not to use their method, which consists of conjecture and the rule of logic, and not to accept their notions, because they corrupt the orthodox faith. The theories of ideas, of no beginning and of everlasting matter, of the eternity of the world, of the pre-existence of souls, of transmigration or reincarnation, of the creation of the world out of existent matter, of the restoration of all things, etc. disturb the teachings of the Church and discredit the Revelation.

b) The theology of the uncreated Light

We mentioned before that the Fathers who wrote the "Synodikon of Orthodoxy" condemned philosophy and its method, as well as those who follow the ancient philosophies and accept their doctrines. But correspondingly they acclaim the holy Fathers, who accepted the truth of the Church and expressed it in their time through their teaching and confession in the Council. I shall not refer to all these topics, but I especially want to emphasise what relates to the theology of the uncreated Light and the distinction between God's essence and energy, because this was one of the most central and basic points in the Councils of the fourteenth century (1341, 1347, 1351) A.D.

Barlaam, a real scholastic theologian of that time, who made use of philosophy at the expense of the vision of God and gave central place to his reasoning and conjecture, as is seen from the tome of the year 1341, maintained that philosophy is superior to theology and to the vision of God. He said that the Light on Mt. Thabor was not unapproachable, nor was it the true light of divinity, nor more holy and divine than the angels, "but even inferior to and lower than this intellect of ours". He said that since that Light falls through the air and strikes the sensory power etc., all the concepts and understandings "are more holy than that light". That light comes and goes, because it is imagined, divided and finite. According to Barlaam, "we rise from such a light (rational) to concepts and visions, which are incomparably better than that light". Therefore he said that anyone who maintains that the Light of the Transfiguration is beyond conceiving and is true and unapproachable "is completely mistaken... irreverent, and so is introducing very pernicious doctrines into the Church".

Barlaam said these things because he had been saturated with the scholastic theology of the West, since he certainly did not even know the theology of the Orthodox Church.

At the same time Barlaam was fighting against the distinction between essence and energy in God, and especially against the teaching of the holy Fathers that God's energy is uncreated.

The orthodox teaching on this subject is set out in the "Synodikon of Orthodoxy". It is said that God has essence and energy and that this distinction does not destroy the divine simplicity. We confess and believe that "uncreated and natural grace and illumination and energy always proceed inseparably from this divine essence". And since, according to the saints, created energy means created essence as well, but uncreated energy characterises uncreated essence", therefore God's energy is uncreated. Indeed the name of divinity is placed not only upon the divine essence, but "also on the divine energy no less". This means that in the teaching of the holy Fathers, "this (the essence) is completely incapable of being shared, but divine grace and energy can be shared".

Likewise in the "Synodikon of Orthodoxy" the truth is presented that the Light of the Transfiguration is not a phantom and a creation, it is not something which appears and then disappears, but it is uncreated and a natural grace and illumination and energy. That is to say, it is the natural glory of divinity. And this Light, which is God's uncreated energy and comes forth indivisibly from the divine essence, appears "through God's benevolence towards those who have purified their nous". So this uncreated light is "light unapproachable... and boundless light and incomprehensible nature of divine radiance, and ineffable glory, and Divinity, supremely perfect glory and beyond perfection, and timeless glory of the Son, and kingdom of God, and true beauty, and lovely in its divine and blessed nature, and natural glory of God, the Father and Spirit flashing forth in the Only-begotten Son, and divinity...".

The holy Fathers are acclaimed who confess "the divine energy proceeding from the divine essence, proceeding undividedly, and because of this proceeding, the ineffable distinction of the things present, but because of the 'undividedly', the marvellous union of the things shown".

And finally the heretics who accept such erroneous views, opposed to the teaching of the holy and god-bearing Fathers, are anathematised. By contrast, the holy Fathers who express unerringly the teaching of the Catholic Orthodox Church are acclaimed and pronounced blessed. Specifically St. Gregory Palamas, Bishop of Thessaloniki, is praised. He is praised for two reasons. One because he successfully confronted and defeated the heretics, who were teaching erroneous ideas about these crucial theological subjects and were attempting to introduce into the Church of Christ "the Platonic ideas and those Greek myths". The other reason is because he set forth the orthodox teaching on these subjects, using all the holy Fathers from Athanasius the Great to his time as interpreters. So here St. Gregory Palamas is presented as a successor to the holy Fathers and champion of the teaching of the Orthodox Church, and for this reason his name is given special and particular mention in the "Synodikon".

The tome of the Synod of 1347 A.D. writes something very important about the value and authority of St. Gregory Palamas and all those monks who follow his teaching. It characterises him as most worthy. And since it anathematises all who do not accept his teaching and oppose him, it says at the same time that if anyone else is ever caught either thinking or speaking or writing against the authority of the said very worthy priestmonk Gregory Palamas and the monks with him, and still more against the holy theologians and this Church, we cast our vote against him, whether he be a priest or a layman". That is to say, whoever speaks against St. Gregory Palamas and his teaching receives excommunication by the Synod. And indeed it is written that we hold St. Gregory Palamas and the monks who agree with him to be not only superior to those against him, or still more, to those sophistries against the Church of God..., but we state that they are protectors of the Church and contenders for the right faith and procurers and helpers of it"[13].

Since even today there are some "theologians" who doubt the teaching of St. Gregory Palamas and regard it as neo-Platonic, let us listen to the excommunication and anathematisation of the Synod which we have mentioned, and in general of the "Synodikon of Orthodoxy".

c) Hesychasm

The Church's theology which was expressed in the 14th century by St. Gregory Palamas concerning God's uncreated energy and the uncreated Light is closely connected with what is called the hesychastic movement. For a man to attain this experience, vision of the uncreated Light, which is identified with deification, it is not a matter of developing his reasoning and loading his brain with knowledge, but a fruit of his purity, of his nous returning to the heart, and illumination of the nous.

From the acts of the Synodal tome of the year 1341 A.D.

---

13. op. cit.p.270

it appears that Barlaam was disputing the way of life of orthodox monasticism, the so-called hesychastic way. Indeed, this is also seen from the whole teaching of St. Gregory Palamas, especially his refutation of Barlaam's views in his well known work "On behalf of the holy hesychasts". I would like, however, to mention one excerpt from the acts of the Synod of 1341. Barlaam said among other things, "Of the many things with which one would have the right to charge the lecturer on such teaching, I regard nothing worse than the fact that in undertaking to upset the mysteries of the Christians by inhalations he even slanders the Fathers as having previously thought the things that he is teaching now"[14].

In the writings of St. Gregory Palamas we see a continual removal of the false doctrine of this teaching of Barlaam, who was trying to shake the foundations of traditional monasticism.

Barlaam had in view the monasticism of the West, which had abandoned the hesychastic method and was busy with a social activity. In the Middle Ages, through the influence of scholastic theology, action (praxis), which in patristic theology is purification of the heart, is interpreted as mission, and vision, which in the theology of the holy Fathers, is noetic prayer and vision of the uncreated Light, is interpreted as mental conjecture about God.

Indeed, inhaling and exhaling, as well as other methods, are psychotechnical methods by which the attempt is made to free the nous from enslavement to the environment and reasoning, and for it to enter the heart, where its real place is, its natural state, and from there to rise to the vision of God. The basic thing is to be able, through the

---

14. op. cit. p.249

grace of God and one's own effort, to concentrate the nous in the heart. This is what is called hesychasm and the hesychastic movement. It is the so-called noetic hesychia, about which so many holy Fathers wrote. By this method the nous is freed from logic and acquires its natural and supranatural way. Then it is in its natural state.

All the holy Fathers followed the same method, and that is why they ended with the same conclusions. Hesychasm is the only method for man's cure. So there are, on the one hand, the hesychasts throughout the ages, who are the unalloyed theologians, and on the other hand, the antihesychasts, who theologise with their imagination and therefore end in heresies.

In the Synodikon of 1341 A.D. there is a very meaningful and characteristic paragraph. Barlaam is condemned, because he was accusing the monks "concerning the holy prayer that occupied them and was often offered by them". The monks practised prayer and noetic hesychia because, as the whole Tradition also bears witness, it is the appropriate method for concentrating the nous in the heart. The Synod accepts this method, which appears to have been accepted by all the Fathers of the Church.

But at the same time the Synod also condemns all those who accept the same views as Barlaam and make accusation against the monks who try to live in a hesychastic way, because the monks are doing nothing else but adopting the method which the Church has. It says characteristically: "But also if any other one of those under him, or any of those who offend in such things, being subject to this excommunication by our humbleness, is seen to be either speaking or writing blasphemously and with false beliefs against the monks, or still more against this Church, let him be excommunicated and cut off from the holy catholic and apostolic Church of Christ and the orthodox community of Christians"[15].

I consider this to be a very important text and reply to those who not only condemn contemporary hesychastic monasticism, but consider it heretical and pursue every means for liberating themselves from the whole hesychastic tradition and assign it a place among the anthropocentric communities or even general religious conventions of life. The statement that they are cut off from the Church of Christ is fearful.

d) The divinely inspired theologies of the saints and the devout mind of the Church

Anyone who studies the "Synodikon of Orthodoxy" will surely observe, when he comes to the chapters that refer to the heresy of Barlaam and Akindynos, that this phrase occurs six times: "against the God-inspired theology of the saints and the devout mind of the Church". And indeed he will observe that the Synod uses the same phrase in opposing all the heretical views of Barlaam and Akindynos and in referring to the teaching of the Church on this particular subject. The heretics are condemned because they do not believe and do not confess "in accordance with the God-inspired theologies of the saints and the devout mind of the Church".

We must notice that the professions of the saints are characterised as God-inspired. And of course divine inspiration is linked with Revelation. The saints experienced God, they attained experience of divine grace, they knew God personally, they reached Pentecost, they received the

---

15. op. cit. p.254

Revelation and therefore are characterised as divinely inspired and unerring teachers of the Church.

We should underline particularly the method which they used and the way they lived in order to become divinely inspired by grace. This way is hesychasm, which is made explicit in the three stages of spiritual perfection: purification of the heart, illumination of the nous and deification. These deified and God-inspired saints are the Prophets in the Old Testament, the Apostles and the holy Fathers. Therefore the "Synodikon of Orthodoxy" says: "As the Prophets saw, as the Apostles taught, as the Church received, as the Teachers laid down as doctrine, as the World has agreed, as grace has shone". So there is identity of what has been experienced by all the saints, precisely because they followed the same method, they experienced the whole mystery of the Cross, which is our flight from sin, the flight of sin from within us and the ascent to the vision of God.

Furthermore, the divinely inspired teaching of the saints is closely connected with the devout mind of the Church. The Church produces the saints and the saints express the devout mind of the Church. Saints cannot be thought of apart from the Church and saints are unthinkable who have heretical and erroneous views on serious theological questions.

In the Church, as St. Gregory Palamas says, there are "those initiated by experience" and those who follow and revere these tested ones. Thus if we do not have our own experience on these matters, we must nevertheless follow the teaching of those who see God, the deified and experienced saints. It is only in this way that we have the mind of the Church and the consciousness of the Church. Otherwise we open the path to self-destruction in various ways.

We must constantly believe and confess "in accordance with the divinely inspired theologies of the saints and the devout mind of the Church".

The "Synodikon of Orthodoxy" is an excellent and very concise text which is a summing up of the whole orthodox teaching of our Church. This is why the Church has inserted it in its worship, on the Sunday of Orthodoxy, and it is read in an attitude of attention and prayer. It is a holy text. And we must harmonise with it all our thinking, and above all, our life.

We need to study it closely in order to recognise what constitutes the orthodox faith and orthodox life. And in fact the orthodox way of life is free of scholasticism and moralism. It is hesychastic and theological.

Our positive or negative stand towards this text shows to what extent we are animated by the orthodox mind of the Church or are possessed by scholasticism. We are of the Church insofar as we are of the holy Fathers.

Glossary

Hagiorite: One whose ascetic life is established on the Holy Mountain; from 'hagios'= 'holy', and 'oros'= 'mountain'. Mount Athos is called the Holy Mountain.

Hesychia, Hesychasm, Hesychast: Hesychia means stillness. Hesychasm is the practice of stillness in the presence of God. Those who practise hesychasm are called hesychasts.

Nepsis: the kind of sober-minded vigilance that characterises the ascetic life. It is usually translated as watchfulness. The adjective is NEPTIC.

Panagia: the All-holy one, the name most used for the Mother of God.

Theotokos: the Mother of God, literally, the birth-giver of God.

Other works by the same author

1. A night in the desert of the Holy Mountain, first edition 1991, reprinted 1994, second edition 1995, reprinted 1998, Birth of the Theotokos monastery, p. 200

2. The illness and cure of the soul in the Orthodox Tradition, first edition 1993, reprinted 1994, 1997 Birth of the Theotokos Monastery, p. 202

3. Orthodox Spirituality, first edition 1994, reprinted 1996, Birth of the Theotokos Monastery, p. 112

4. Orthodox Psychotherapy, first edition 1994, reprinted 1995, 1997, Birth of the Theotokos Monastery, p. 372

5. Life after death, first edition 1996, reprinted 1998, Birth of the Theotokos Monastery, p. 392

6. St. Gregory Palamas as a Hagiorite, Birth of the Theotokos Monastery, 1997, p. 400

7. The person in the Orthodox Tradition, Birth of the Theotokos Monastery, 1998

* * *

8. Mia vradia stin erimo tou agiou Orous, editions A' 1978, B' 1979, Γ' 1982, Δ' 1984, E' 1985, ΣΤ' 1986, Z' 1987,

Η' 1989, Θ' 1990, Ι' 1992, ΙΑ' 1993, ΙΒ' 1994, ΙΓ' 1995, ΙΔ' 1997, ΙΕ' 1998, Birth of the Theotokos Monastery

9. Osmi Gnoseos, editions "Tertios", Katerini 1985

10. Martiria zois, 1985

11. To Mistirion tis paedias tou Theou editions A' 1985, B' 1987, Γ' 1991, Δ' 1997, Birth of the Theotokos Monastery

12. Paraklitika, editions "Tertios", Katerini 1986

13. Orthodoxi Psychotherapia (Pateriki therapeutiki agogi) editions A' 1986, B' 1987, Γ' 1989, Δ' 1992, Ε' 1995, ΣΤ' 1998, Birth of the Theotokos Monastery

14. Piotita zois, editions A' 1987, B' 1989, Γ' 1996, Birth of the Theotokos Monastery

15. Apokalipsi tou Theou, editions A' 1987, B' 1992, Γ' 1996, Birth of the Theotokos Monastery

16. Therapeutiki agogi, editions A' 1987, B' 1989, Γ' 1993, Δ' 1998, Birth of the Theotokos Monastery

17. Sizitisis gia tin Orthodoxi Psychotherapia, editions A' 1988, B' 1992, Γ' 1998, Birth of the Theotokos Monastery

18. Psychiki asthenia kai igia, editions A' 1989, B' 1991, Γ' 1995, Birth of the Theotokos Monastery

19. Anatolika I, editions A' 1989, B' 1993, Birth of the Theotokos Monastery

20. Keros tou piisai, Birth of the Theotokos Monastery, 1990

21. To politevma tou Stavrou, editions A' 1990, B' 1992, Birth of the Theotokos Monastery

22. Ecclesiastiko fronima, editions A' 1990, B' 1993, Birth of the Theotokos monastery

23. Prosopo kai Eleftheria, Birth of the Theotokos Monastery, 1991

24. O Vlepon, editions A' 1991, B' 1992, Birth of the Theotokos Monastery

25. Orthodoxos kai ditikos tropos zois, editions A' 1992, B' 1994, Birth of the Theotokos Monastery

26. Mikra isodos stin Orthodoxi pnevmatikotita, Athens 1992

27. O Agios Grigorios o Palamas os Agioritis, editions A' 1992, B' 1996, Birth of the Theotokos Monastery

28. Katichisi kai Baptisi ton enilikon, Athens 1993

29. Romeoi se Anatoli kai Disi, Birth of the Theotokos Monastery, 1993

30. Paremvasis stin sychroni kinonoia A', Birth of the Theotokos Monastery, 1994

31. Paremvasis stin sychroni kinonoia B', Birth of the Theotokos Monastery, 1994

32. AIDS, enas tropos zois, 1994

33. To prosopo stin Orthodoxi Paradosi, editions B' 1994, Γ' 1997, Birth of the Theotokos Monastery

34. Epoptiki Katichisi, Birth of the Theotokos Monastery, 1994

35. I zoi meta ton thanato, editions A' 1994, B' 1995, Γ' 1996, Δ' 1997, Birth of the Theotokos Monastery

36. I Despotikes eortes, Birth of the Theotokos Monastery, 1995

37. Iparxiaki psychologia kai Orthodoxi Psychotherapia, editions A' 1995, B' 1997, Birth of the Theotokos Monastery

38. Osoi pistoi, Birth of the Theotokos Monastery, 1996

39. Gennima kai thremma Romeoi, Birth of the Theotokos Monastery, 1996

40. Entefxis kai synentefxis, Birth of the Theotokos Monastery, 1997

41. Ikonofiliko kai Iconoclastiko pnevma, Birth of the Theotokos Monastery, 1998

* * *

42. Secularism in church, theology and pastoral care, "The truth", ἀρ. φύλ. 11, 29 Μαΐου - 5 Ἰουνίου 1994, W. Australia and "Alive in Christ", the magazine of the Diocese of Eastern Pennsylvania, Orthodoxy Church in America, Volume X, No 1, 2, 1994, καί Divine ascent, a journal of Orthodox faith, exaltation of the Holy Cross 1997, Vol. 1, No. 2, p. 10-25

43. Die Autorität in der orthodoxen Kirche (Kurzfassung der Einführung für deutsche Theologiestudenten am

29.9.1996), εἰς Philia, Zeitschrift für wissenschaftliche,
ökumenische und kulturelle Zusammenarbeit der Grie-
chisch-Deutschen Initiative, II/1996

44. СЕКУЛАРИЗАМ У ЦРКВИ, БОГОСЛОВЉУ И
ПАСТИРСКОМ РАДУ, СВЕТИ ГОРА, τεῦχος 68,
69, 1998

45. ВОСКРЕСЕНИЕ ХРИСТОВО, Крым 1998